DAUNTLESS MARINE

Joseph Sailer Jr., Dive-Bombing Ace of Guadalcanal

DAUNTLESS MARINE

Joseph Sailer Jr., Dive-Bombing Ace of Guadalcanal

Alexander S. White

White Knight Press
Fairfax Station, Virginia

Printed in the United States of America

Book production by Farragut Publishing Company, Washington, D.C.
Jacket design by Eason Associates, Washington, D.C.
First printing 1996

Library of Congress Catalog Card Number 95-62271
ISBN 0-9649875-0-3

To the memory of my mother

CONTENTS

Preface ix

Note on Sources and Acknowledgments xiii

Chapter One: The Family 1

Chapter Two: The Thirties 21

Chapter Three: Sperry 41

Chapter Four: Preparing for War 61

Chapter Five: Guadalcanal 71

Chapter Six: November–December 1942 91

Chapter Seven: Aftermath 107

Chapter Eight: Final Thoughts 129

Appendix A 133

Appendix B 137

Appendix C 139

Notes 141

Bibliography 163

Index 167

PREFACE

Growing up in Philadelphia, I occasionally heard my mother speak about her brother, my Uncle Joe. Over the years I learned two things about him: he had been a very good person, and he had been killed in World War II, several years before I was born, at a place called Guadalcanal. There were a few books about the war in the Pacific on our bookshelves, and I once or twice looked in their indexes and saw that Joseph Sailer Jr. was mentioned several times in these volumes. As I grew older I kept in the back of my mind the interesting fact that my uncle had been successful enough in the war to be written about in several books, but I did not make any effort to discover further details about his career or his life, of which I knew practically nothing.

Several events motivated me to take a different attitude toward Uncle Joe's life. The appearance of a genetic disorder in my family caused me to develop an interest in genealogy, at first in order to trace the family's ethnic background, and later for the general enjoyment of family history research. Then, in 1992, when my mother was stricken with cancer, I spent some time talking to her about her family, including Uncle Joe. She mentioned again, as she had a few other times over the years, that there was a chest full of his papers and personal effects that she would like me to have eventually. After she died later that year, I took possession of the chest and everything else concerning him that I could locate.

The chest sat undisturbed for about six months. Then my wife, Clenise, happened to mention to a business acquaintance, Jack Monroe, that I had these materials and was considering putting together some sort of history of my uncle's career with the Marine Corps. Jack is a retired Marine Corps colonel and an official with the Marine Corps Aviation Association in Quantico, Virginia. He sent us a copy of John McEniry's excellent book, *A Marine Dive-Bomber Pilot at Guadalcanal*, which was dedicated in part to Uncle Joe by the author, a pilot in my uncle's squadron at Guadalcanal. Jack also suggested that I run an advertisement in "The Yellow Sheet," the association's quarterly newsletter, seeking information from those who knew Uncle Joe in the Marine Corps. I did this, not expecting much response.

When the new issue of "The Yellow Sheet" appeared in the summer of 1993, our phone started ringing. There was just one problem—through a mixup the announcement had included our fax number rather than our regular phone number. For two or three days we heard that line ringing, certain that veterans of Guadalcanal were trying to reach me with their recollections of Uncle Joe. We tried to pick up the line, but the fax machine took over.

Eventually we fixed the problem so that other callers could get through, and I'm confident I ultimately contacted everyone who had tried to call earlier. The response to that announcement was amazing, and was what really got this project off the ground. Encouraged because there were so many veterans willing to share their stories with me, I decided the time was right to take all of the written material I had, gather what oral information I could, and put it all together in a form to record the story of Uncle Joe's life for the current generation and those to come.

My grandmother apparently had saved every piece of paper relating to Uncle Joe that was still in existence when he died. There are letters he had written as early as 1918, when he was eleven, and as late as September 1942, just over two months before he was killed—108 in all. There is a much smaller number of letters written to him, and most of those, through some working of chance, are from 1937. There also are a considerable number of letters written to his mother by relatives, friends, and military colleagues after his death, some of them quite informative.

The chest also contained many photographs, some of which are reproduced here, several newspaper and magazine articles about the fighting at Guadalcanal, and a few other items of considerable interest, such as a partial diary for 1931, a passport, pilot's licenses, and Uncle Joe's aviator's log book covering the period from March 1938 through his final flight. Using these materials as the framework for his life story, I attempted to fill in the gaps as best I could.

The letters revealed that Guadalcanal was not the only scene of my uncle's wartime activity. The documents also contained cryptic references to events that had taken place in England. I had not known about this aspect of Uncle Joe's career, and because of the secrecy involved during the war, it was somewhat more challenging to discover the details of this particular mission. Eventually I learned that in late 1940 he had been sent to England with one or more bomb sights made by his employer, the Sperry Gyroscope

Company. The story of this mission, which was a deep secret at the time, provides some interesting insight into a little-known aspect of the aid provided by the United States to England in the early years of the war.

My purpose in this book is to provide a full picture of the life of Joseph Sailer Jr., not to provide a non-expert's views on the fighting in the Pacific or other aspects of the war. I have attempted to present an account of Uncle Joe's most significant actions in the war, and to clear up a few minor inaccuracies in some of the books and articles that mentioned him. I have not uncovered much new information about the military action at Guadalcanal apart from a few facts such as the identity of the gunner who flew on my uncle's final mission.

The story of Uncle Joe's life as presented here is not complete. There are many gaps in the periods covered by his letters, and, unfortunately, there are no letters, diaries, or other material written by him from Guadalcanal. Where there are uncertainties, I have been careful not to invent or reconstruct actions or thoughts, no matter how likely they might seem. (I also have not corrected my uncle's spelling, which was one area in which he did not excel.) If this approach makes the narrative less compelling, I hope the reader will accept my choice to prefer accuracy over drama. Uncle Joe's life was well endowed with actual adventure and accomplishment, and I have attempted to let the facts of his story speak for themselves.

NOTE ON SOURCES AND ACKNOWLEDGMENTS

Besides the letters and other items preserved in the family archives, I relied on numerous sources of information. I was fortunate enough to locate several members of my uncle's squadron at Guadalcanal, including Archie "Hap" Simpson, who was on his wing on the final flight; L.B. Robertshaw, his executive officer; and Howard Stanley, who was the radio-gunner for every one of his combat flights at Guadalcanal except the final one. All of these men, and several others, were extraordinarily helpful in answering my questions. The names of those I contacted are set out in the bibliography, and I am very grateful to them for their patience in helping me reconstruct the details of my uncle's career.

In piecing together the story of my uncle's trip to England in 1940 I had no idea at first how to proceed based on the cryptic references in his letters and other papers. Then I tried posting a query on a military discussion forum of CompuServe, an online computer service. Within a few days I received a response from a military enthusiast directing me to Bombardiers, Inc., an organization in Alabama devoted to preserving the history of World War II bombardiers and their missions and equipment. This organization provided me with excellent information on the Sperry bomb sight, and put me in touch with Dr. Carl Frische, a former president of Sperry.

As it turned out, Dr. Frische had known Uncle Joe quite well, and was able to answer many questions about the trip to England. He also referred me to Franklin Joseph, the Sperry engineer who had relieved Uncle Joe in England. Mr. Joseph, an avid family historian himself, had written his own account of his trip overseas in connection with the bomb sights. What is more, he was able to track down one of the most elusive items in my quest for information. In several of the letters in the chest, there were references to a documentary film called "Experiences in England," produced by Sperry and relating the story of the company's efforts with the bomb sight overseas in 1940 and 1941. I had no idea if any copies of this 1942 film still existed, but Franklin Joseph managed to track down a surviving sixteen-millimeter print and have it transferred to videotape. The film is itself a fascinating document, and it provided several valuable revelations about Uncle Joe's trip. I never could have solved the mysteries of that trip without the incredibly generous assistance of Franklin Joseph and Carl Frische.

Uncle Joe's life, of course, did not consist solely of military service and his work for Sperry. I found out as much as I could from his sisters, my aunts Alice and Priscilla (augmenting what I had already learned from my mother), and then tried to track down others who had known him at various stages in his life. Through the alumni offices at Chestnut Hill Academy and Princeton University I made contact with classmates from the classes of 1926 and 1930, respectively, who provided me with some good information. I did not succeed in speaking to any of the women Uncle Joe had dated, unfortunately. I located one woman with whom Uncle Joe had carried on considerable correspondence and who was considered by some (not necessarily by him) as a prime candidate to be his wife. I wrote her a letter asking if she would be willing to talk to me. A few weeks later I received a very nice reply from her sister, saying the lady in question had recently been hospitalized with a serious illness, but would be very glad to speak to me about her "good friend Joe Sailer" when she recovered. I regret to say that I never heard from her further.

Similarly, I would have loved to contact Floy Larsen, who stored Uncle Joe's car for him when he was preparing to leave Quantico, Virginia, to go off to the war, and who wrote several very interesting letters to his mother after he was killed. I have been unsuccessful in locating her, perhaps because of a change in her last name upon marriage. Remarkably enough, I did locate at least two other individuals named Floy Larsen, but neither was the one I was looking for. It is my hope that some readers of this account may help me locate Miss Larsen and several other persons mentioned in the narrative whose trails I could not follow.

In researching my uncle's service in World War II, although I have consulted original military records, such as the war diaries of the aviation squadrons, I have made no attempt to make any original assessment or interpretation of the military events that took place at Guadalcanal. For the military significance of what took place, I have relied on the excellent accounts written by authors such as Richard Frank, John Lundstrom, Thomas Miller, and several others, which are cited in the notes and the bibliography.

Beyond the material mentioned above, I managed to track down a good many facts through ordinary library research. I am fortunate to live near Washington, D.C., with access to the Library of Congress, the National Archives, the Marine Corps Historical Center, and other valuable repositories of military history. Jack Monroe and others affiliated with the Marine Corps Aviation Association were a great source of encouragement, support, and information.

Finally, several relatives and others provided me with important assistance in getting this book written. My brother and sister-in-law, Welsh and Linda White, and my cousins Priscilla Wilson and John Churchman dug up very useful documents among the family papers. My mother-in-law, Josephine Stonitsch, did a superb job of transcribing many hours of tape-recorded interviews and the soundtrack of the Sperry film. My brother-in-law, Michael Zkiab, did valuable research for me at the Public Record Office in England. My nephew, Paul Zkiab, did a wonderful job of producing the artwork on the back cover according to my request. Daniel Rapoport, Merideth Menken, and Elizabeth Webber of Farragut Publishing Company patiently and expertly guided me through the intricacies of turning a manuscript and a group of photographs into a finished product. Becky Eason and Ted Lopez did a superb job of designing the cover. Above all, my wife Clenise has been as always an enduring inspiration. Without her optimism and support I never could have completed this work.

CHAPTER ONE
THE FAMILY

Throughout his life, including most of his military career, Joseph Sailer Jr. maintained strong ties with his family. Whether he was serving at far-flung military bases or carrying out a secret mission to England before the United States entered World War II, he never stayed out of touch for long with his mother and his six brothers and sisters. (His father died when Joe was twenty-one.) In a sense he lived a dual existence; some people who worked very closely with him at the Sperry Gyroscope Company and in the military expressed surprise years later when they learned that their colleague had any living relatives at all. He did not readily mix the two sides of his life, and he did not share his innermost thoughts with those he worked with. As a consequence, the men who knew Major Joe Sailer in 1942 as a greatly respected squadron leader at Guadalcanal, and as one of the most outstanding dive-bomber pilots of the war, knew little of the background that preceded his final assignment.

His reticence about his personal life did not mean that he had anything to hide; Sailer's story is not that of a man who was toughened by a difficult childhood or who overcame adversities by finding a place in the military. Quite

1

the contrary: He came from an affluent family that gave him much, from a fine education to a strong moral code. Few forces were as important to the molding of his character as the influence of his family, both as a group of individuals who contributed specific lessons or ideas and as a general source of codes of conduct and attitudes towards life. It is impossible to understand this quiet, unassuming Marine without spending some time looking at his roots.

With the advantages that accompany affluence and privilege, the family that Joe Sailer was born into in 1907 had forged strong and lasting ties over the generations; young children spent time not just with parents and siblings but with a wide variety of uncles, great-aunts, grandparents, and first and second cousins. There were home bases in large houses in the city and what was then the "country" (now the semiurban Philadelphia neighborhoods of Germantown and Mt. Airy). In the summers, beginning sometime in the late nineteenth century, the women and children headed up to family retreats on the coast of New England; the men would join them for whatever weeks they could get away from work. There were live-in domestic workers to do much of the cooking, cleaning, and child care. In this congenial and insulated environment, Joe, like his siblings, came to have a great rapport with many members of the extended family on both sides of his deeply rooted family tree.

Joe's mother, Mary Lowber Strawbridge, was descended from eighteenth-century Irish and English immigrants, some of whom settled at first on the Eastern Shore of Maryland. Joe's great-great-great grandfather, John Strawbridge (one of several with this name), born in Ireland in 1749, immigrated to America, where he became sheriff of a Maryland county and a major in the militia. According to family records, in August 1777 he happened to discover that the British under General Howe were approaching in ships by way of the Chesapeake Bay, rather than by the Delaware River, as General Washington had expected. He carried this news to Washington's camp, whereupon he was asked to accompany Washington and Lafayette to the top of Iron Hill, near Elkton, Maryland, from which the generals, "by the aid of glasses," could see the British fleet. According to the papers of the son of John Strawbridge, "Washington was highly pleased with my father and before they separated urged him to accept a captain's commission in the continental army. This compliment he was compelled under all circumstances respectfully to decline."

Later Strawbridges moved on to Wilmington, Delaware, and Philadelphia. John Strawbridge, the one-time adviser to George Washington, and Major Joe Sailer's great-great-great-grandfather, moved in 1783 from Elkton, Maryland, to Philadelphia, where he became a successful merchant with a store near the Delaware River waterfront. These Philadelphia roots grew thick and sturdy over the next several generations. John Strawbridge's grandson, George, was a very successful ophthalmologist in the city, and a leading figure in real estate and civic affairs. Although not the only source of his descendants' relative affluence, he was one of the primary accumulators of family wealth. After his death in 1914, his widow Alice sold one of his prime real estate holdings, a lot at 13th and Chestnut streets in the heart of center-city Philadelphia's commercial district, for about $600,000, at that time a record price.[1]

Alice Welsh Strawbridge herself came from a distinguished background; her father, John Welsh, was appointed minister to the Court of St. James by President Hayes in 1877. He served in that capacity in England until 1879. A noted philanthropist, he managed the finances of Philadelphia's Centennial celebration of 1876; he was eulogized as "the Foremost of Philadelphia's Citizens" upon his death in 1886.[2] Alice Welsh was born July 24, 1848, at her grandparents' "country" estate, Spring Bank, in the Mt. Airy section of Philadelphia, off Wissahickon Avenue. One of John Welsh's descendants described the place many years ago in matter-of-fact prose that still manages to evoke the fairy-tale aura of a fine and pleasant retreat where the family could live according to its own standard of comfort and stately solace:

> It [Spring Bank] embraces many broad acres of hill and dale with pasture, stream and woodlands. There is a row of oaks along the roadway in front that add grandeur to the beauty of the undulating lawn, that falls and then rises back to the buildings beyond. There is a double entrance; the lower driveway leads to the house, the upper to the stable, with connecting link half way. A grassy circle of well-kept turf shaded by one large coffee tree divides the driveway before the final curve is reached. The old fashioned house, three stories with kitchen added on the southern slope, is homelike in appearance. The lower porch, the summer sitting room, is at the rear. The enclosed upper porch of equal dimensions is the children's playground in wet weather. Guarding both on the

lawn nearby is an immense tulip poplar. The tennis court and pasture intervene. Then come the woods beyond. In the valley below the springhouse is a pond fed by springs. The overflow seeks its level in the Wissahickon Valley. The chestnut grove, the pride of the place, is on the hill beyond the stream.

On the other side are the flower garden, the vegetable garden separated by a wall, the orchard and the cherry trees where lovers sit and view the vista over the Wissahickon. Far away, behind them, are the gardener's house, the stables, the greenhouse, and the outbuildings. . . .

Spring Bank possessed the first lawn tennis set ever brought to this country from England. Spring Bank's lawn tennis was the scene of the first tennis tournament played in America.[3]

George and Alice Welsh Strawbridge, who married in 1873, had six children. Mary Lowber Strawbridge was born July 4, 1875, not at Spring Bank, but at The Wilderness, a residence across the street, stately and spacious, though not so grand as Spring Bank. Mary, like all members of the extended family, was well instructed by nurses and parents in the rules of behavior and the manners that were of such critical importance to success in her environment of ladies and gentlemen, of dance classes where the young men wore white gloves, and of fine private schools where young ladies were taught that "horses sweat, and men perspire, but ladies only glow."

Her only sister who survived infancy was eight years younger, so Mary had to fend for herself in a world dominated by her three brothers and other boys. She had spunk and energy enough to survive very well; she rode horses, went on sleigh rides, and in proper course made her debut into society, a graceful, slender blonde with sparkling light-blue eyes. Although she didn't stray so far from custom for young ladies near the turn of the century as to attend four years of college, she did take some courses in chemistry at Drexel University, and taught for a while. Meanwhile, because her mother was retiring and shied away from active social life, Mary took the initiative and put on parties for herself. As she reached the age for marriage, the only respectable option other than spinsterhood, she became engaged to William Lloyd, a third cousin. But this match arose from the inevitability of matrimony, rather than from the spark of passion, and Mary was not one to tread unblinking down a mistaken course. Through a fine symmetry of intersecting lives, she met a dark and handsome doctor named Joseph Sailer, who had been practicing medicine for about a decade, and had recently spent three years studying abroad, primarily in Zurich, Paris, and Vienna. Although he was then engaged to a European woman and Mary was still betrothed to Mr. Lloyd, the force of their attraction overcame these impediments. Two engagements were broken and the Sailer and Strawbridge families merged.

Born October 1, 1867, Doctor Joseph Sailer was eight years senior to Miss Strawbridge. He, too, came from a prominent Philadelphia family. His father, John Sailer, had served as an officer of the Keystone Battery in the Civil War, and then went on to form a successful banking firm, Sailer & Stevenson. John's father, also named Joseph Sailer, was for many years the financial editor of a major newspaper, the *Philadelphia Public Ledger*, and was considered one of the top financial experts in the country.[4] John Sailer was very active in civic affairs, serving as a director of various banks, businesses, and other institutions. He and his wife, Emily Woodward, had two sons and two daughters: Emily, Nancy, John, and Joseph.

Joseph's affinity for scholarship showed itself early; he enrolled in the University of Pennsylvania at fourteen, and graduated at eighteen from the biological department with the degree of Bachelor of Philosophy. John Sailer, however, was not interested in having his son pursue the field of medical study that already was calling to the precocious youngster; banking had been good to the father, and he strongly desired that his son follow the family calling. He insisted that Joseph work in the family bank for two years.

But Joseph, like his future wife, knew himself well enough to avoid an unfulfilling path, and had the backbone to steer himself decisively away from it. He quit the bank and pursued a career in the discipline he loved; he received his Doctor of Medicine degree from the University of Pennsylvania in 1891. After his internship in Philadelphia and study in Europe, he settled into the practice and teaching of clinical medicine, eventually establishing himself as a highly respected diagnostician, with special interests in gastroenterology, cardiology, and neurology. During World War I he served as a lieutenant colonel in the United States Marine Corps, first as a doctor at Camp Wheeler in Macon, Georgia, and then as a medical consultant at Vichy, France. Upon his return from the war, he expressed to the press his indignation at what he saw as blatant mistreatment of American prisoners who were repatriated through the American Hospital Center at Vichy: "Either the Germans were exceedingly poor surgeons or else they deliberately mishandled our wounded in their prison camps."[5]

After Joseph and Mary married on February 5, 1901, they settled into a small but comfortable townhouse with a little garden on the roof in center-city Philadelphia at 208 South 21st Street. As they settled into married life they had a firm sense of *noblesse oblige*—of the responsibilities that their privileged background imposed on them.

Their first child came without delay, in March 1902. Emily was a vital spark of childish energy; she grew to preschool age as a cherished companion and friend to her parents. Alice followed soon after, in April 1904, and Mary (who, as a child, called herself "Mary, Jr.") in January 1906. When Mary was only a few weeks old, in March 1906, the Sailers faced the first, and perhaps the greatest, shock of their lives together. Their darling Emily, just turned four years old, in the full blush of her innocent girlhood, died of pneumonia despite what was probably the best medical care available anywhere in the country. Mary and Joseph managed their grief by pouring out their precious memories of Emily in a flood of words; they each kept a journal in the weeks after their daughter's death, in which they recorded every detail they could remember of the many little joys of their lost angel's short life. But they did not have unlimited time for reminiscences; the young family had another addition in little more than a year.

Joseph Sailer Jr. was born August 14, 1907, during the family's summer stay at the seashore, which this year was in Jamestown, Rhode Island, rather than Camden, Maine, which later would become the perennial summer destination. Joe had two ready-made playmates in Alice and Mary, and, within two years, he was joined by the Sailers' second son, John, born in June 1909. They ultimately would get a third brother, Albin Penington (called Pen), but not until December 1913. Sisters Priscilla and Elizabeth (Betty) came along in between, in 1910 and 1912. The full set of ten children was completed by two sisters, Anne West and Virginia, born in 1916 and 1920, both of whom died in early childhood. To accommodate the growing family, the Sailers moved twice: to 1830 Spruce Street in 1908, and, in 1916, to 1718 Spruce Street, where the family was to have its home base until 1942.

Joe was a cute, blond little fellow with blue eyes and a pleasant disposition that would win him loyal friends throughout his life. His childhood was uneventful and happy as far as can be told, apart from the normal family crises and an occasional shock of nature, not so rare in that era, such as the death of his five-year-old little sister, Anne West, in 1922. He was exposed to the full range of opportunities made possible by his birth into an affluent family, from horseback riding to golf and tennis. One of the strongest forces that fed his character, though, must have flowed from the family's annual summer vacations in a majestic setting on the New England coast.

Mary Sailer's parents, Dr. George Strawbridge and Alice Welsh Strawbridge, like many of their peers, regularly retreated from the oppressive, wilting heat and humidity of Philadelphia summers to a placid seaside resort in Maine. Probably beginning around the turn of the century, the destination for the Strawbridges was Rockledge, their summer "cottage" on the rock-bound coast at Camden, on the Belfast Road (now U.S. Route 1) in the mid-coastal region of the state. They gathered their children and grandchildren with them in a part of the world that was, in some ways, more precious to the family members than their permanent place of residence 500 miles to the south.

Camden is a picturesque town, blessed with ancient arrangements of natural features that cooperate to soothe the city-weary traveler with views of green trees on compact mountains of gray rock. These Camden Hills are juxtaposed with a little curving harbor filled with colorful sailboats and lobstering craft. Dominating the main street of a few blocks of shops and businesses is Mount Battie, a mountain-hill that rises abruptly from the edge of the harbor to a flat summit of about 800 feet. A few miles outside of the town, a narrow road leads into the dark woods surrounding Lake Megunticook, lying in the shelter of the Camden Hills. Nowhere wider than a few hundred yards, but miles in length, the lake in its isolated stillness offers a timeless respite to the fortunate inhabitants of the hundreds of summer cabins and cottages, some primitive and some quite grand, that stand on virtually every part of its shores.

In the early 1900s, Camden offered these charms each summer to the Strawbridges and to the young Sailer family, who partook of them with delight and a sense of easy familiarity. In the earliest years of the century, including 1907, the year Joe was born, the Sailers spent summers in Jamestown, Rhode Island. Before long, though, the Sailers began going to Camden every summer, staying at first in rented houses. They eventually bought their own place, the Forecastle—a spacious Victorian cottage of dark green wood that overlooked Penobscot Bay from the peak of Chestnut Street through a peaceful frame of rich Maine trees. It is a solid, comfortable house still—one of great character in a location with qualities of beauty and enchantment that cannot have failed to instill in those who spent their summers there a lasting love of nature, life, and the sea.

The summer in Maine must have been the highlight of the year for many of the Sailers. Mary and the children would take the train up from Philadelphia sometime in June; they would remain in Camden until August. Joseph would join them for whatever time he could steal from his medical practice. Some of the children would spend at least part of the time with their grandmother Strawbridge in her place out on the Belfast Road; the others would be with their mother in town at the Forecastle. There always were plenty of activities for children; a great diversity of relatives and friends flowed through the family properties. In one of the earliest surviving letters written by Joe Sailer, sent to his father probably during World War I when he was about ten, the boy noted that his uncle Albin Sailer had driven up the day before; and there were "a great number of boys up hear that live around are house so we can have quiet a number of games together."[6] Also, "Aunt" (probably his mother's sister Anne West Strawbridge) was there, so Joe, his sister Mary, brother John, and his mother took his aunt for a walk around the seaside golf course at the Megunticook Golf Club. They then had a drive in his Granny's automobile. During the afternoons, the family was teaching Joe's little sister Priscilla how to swim in the lake.

Through the early 1920s, the Sailers had the benefit of the Strawbridges' place as well as their own, and Joe was active in both locations. When he was about sixteen, he rode a motorcycle, with his brother John on the rear end, down the long driveway to Rockledge. He was doing fine until the brakes failed. He showed his resourcefulness and

11

ability to keep a calm head; he guided the runaway cycle off to the nearest field and kept riding around in circles until he could bring it to a stop. The resulting rut was a visible feature for a long time thereafter.[7]

Lake Megunticook, where the family often would spend afternoons at their cottage (in this case a more apt term) by the water, was another idyllic retreat. The little cabin had a single bathroom and a somewhat primitive kitchen, with running water drawn directly from the lake. Perhaps the most important features on the property were the bathhouse and the floating wooden platform connected to the shore by a ramp. From this float, the children could swim and dive and dry off in the summer sun as they listened to the lapping of the water underneath the creaking gray boards. There were at times over the years many types of equipment for the children and adults alike to enjoy, including rowboats, kayaks, and canoes. Time seemed to stand still; the everyday world did not intrude into this scene of calm waters resting at the foot of the mountains of Camden. For many of the children, the daily trips to the lake were the high point of their time in Maine. Joe Sailer certainly loved those times; over the years he would try to get up there every summer if at all possible. If he couldn't, he still would think of ways to improve the fun of his relatives who were there.

Apart from the beach and the lake, there were climbs up the steep but short Mount Battie, and the other Camden Hills, such as Mount Megunticook and Bald Rock. On one occasion in August 1918, Mary Sailer, with her sister Anne West Strawbridge and her children Mary, Joe, and John, climbed Mount Battie just two days after Colonel Theodore Roosevelt had ascended it in a car; the Sailer family saw the tire tracks. Around this time, Joe and his mother played tennis just about every day; she thought he did quite well for a beginner.[8] Alice preferred to play golf. In Camden Harbor, in classes at the Camden Yacht Club, Joe, his siblings, and a multitude of other relatives took up sailing, a sport in which he was to achieve considerable expertise.

The summers were not spent wholly in physical exercise and recreation. Joseph Sr. was firmly of the opinion that young minds had to be exercised throughout the year; it was not proper to while away the entire season without some mental discipline. So, during perhaps three summers, including that of 1917, Joe and his sisters Alice and Mary walked from the Forecastle to a small house at 12 Limerock Street, a few blocks down the tree-lined hill of Chestnut Street. There they were tutored in Latin, history, and possibly other subjects by a young woman who was already one of the country's best-known poets—Edna St. Vincent Millay, who was to become the first American woman to win the Pulitzer Prize for poetry. Miss Millay, along with her sisters Norma and Kathleen, needed the money from tutoring, or at least felt compelled to earn it.[9] It was probably Mount Megunticook whose spectacular vantage point had been the inspiration for the opening lines of "Renascence," the poem that in 1912 launched the career of the energetic girl who scrambled up the mountain before dawn just to enjoy the beauties of nature:

All I could see from where I stood
Was three long mountains and a wood;
I turned and looked another way,
And saw three islands in a bay.

The Sailer children may not have been suitably impressed by the poet's stature, though; during one of the tutoring sessions, after Miss Millay had recited her famous poem about burning the candle at both ends, Joe's sister Mary, about eleven years old at the time, announced her view that the poem was no good at all.[10]

Back in the more mundane life of Philadelphia, Joe attended excellent all-boys' private schools. For the early grades he studied at the William Penn Charter School in Germantown, which boasted a rich Quaker heritage. In 1919, he transferred to Chestnut Hill Academy, located in a former resort hotel in a peaceful, suburban setting sheltered by magnificent trees, still within the city but out in the farthest northwest fork, even beyond The Wilderness and Spring Bank. The graduating class had only fifteen students, including Joe's cousin, John Strawbridge Jr. (Jack). Although Joe started out with the class of 1925, he graduated with the class of 1926, just one year ahead of his brother John. The 1926 yearbook awarded Sailer the label of "quietest" in the class, a rating belied by his participation as a letterman in varsity football, track, and basketball, in the latter as captain in his two final years. He was by no means a musclebound athlete; the yearbook shows him, at age eighteen, as standing five feet ten inches and weighing 135 pounds.

During the high school years, Sailer was known as a very responsible, reliable sort of fellow, who didn't excel in academics but never had trouble with his studies. He was seen as dependable, and was very well respected; he had a rather serious image, but he "didn't throw his weight around." On the football field, he had a reputation as being steady and someone you could count on when the going got tough.[11] One of his classmates recalled how Joe, as basketball captain, had rallied the team from a 12–1 deficit at halftime to win the game in overtime.[12]

Accompanied by Jack Strawbridge and several other classmates, Sailer went on to Princeton, where he joined the Princeton Quadrangle Club, majored in mechanical engineering, and kept a fairly low profile, not going out for varsity sports. He did very well in his engineering studies, but not well in subjects such as French and economics. His classmates remembered him for his unflappable good humor and complete absence of meanness. He was known for being patriotic, respectful of women, and maybe "just a little bit shy."[13] One characteristic that was to be of great importance in later life was evident during the college years. Charles Stephenson, one of his friends from the Quadrangle Club, remarked years later:

> [H]e was a very compelling person. . . . You could see, here was a man that's all of one piece. He was self-contained. He had total control of himself.[14]

Stephenson also recalled Joe's other most noticeable traits:

> [He] was just a happy, congenial, fun-loving member of our class and our Quadrangle contingent. He was serious minded about his studies. He had a strict code of proper behavior, and gentlemanly traits. He was every inch a gentleman. He was very thoughtful of others. He wanted to make a decent record at Princeton, but never at the expense of anyone else. He never pushed anyone aside so he could get ahead. . . . Everybody

liked Joe Sailer; there wasn't a man or girl who had any dislike of Joe. He was kind and respectful to everybody, not only to the elderly, but to his peers. . . . [H]e would make a whole room feel better, a whole room full of people, without even trying, and there wasn't anything ostentatious about this.[15]

His time at college appears to have been happy and productive, and it was the time when he seems to have realized what he most wanted to do with his life. One day he was walking on campus with Charlie Stephenson when a barnstormer's biplane, a Waco, buzzed overhead. Joe turned to Charlie with innocent wonder and enthusiasm. "Gosh," he said, or words to that effect, "look at that fellow flying up there, soaring like an eagle. Now that's what I would really like to do." It isn't clear if the seed of passion for aviation had been planted in him earlier, but there is no doubt that, while he was at college, Joe knew that he wanted to fly, probably as a career.

Before he could realize this dream, though, he had to endure another loss. One of the few surviving records of these years is a letter, made poignant by its timing, that Joe wrote to his ailing father from college in October 1928:

Dear Daddy,

I was sorry not to be home on your birthday as I guess you had a fine party with lots of presents. I don't know whether or not you remember or not but when you said good-bye to me before I caught my train last Sunday you told me that you wanted me to work very hard at my lessons. I find, however, that you have asked me to do a very hard thing as you ought not to expect a son of yours to feel that it is all right for him to be in college spending your money if you feel that you have to work to send him there. I myself don't think that it is necessary as John and I figured out what the family income is and it ought to be pleanty if we live on an economical basis. Of course, you would know much more about such matters than I would but just the same there is no reason why we should not spend a little of our principle if that were necessary (which I don't think it is) while you took a good rest. If I had any power over you I would make you stop all of your heavy & tiresome work and just go to a few consultations a week. Next summer you could buy a small yacht and we could have some swell cruises together. This may sound absurd to you but after all we are far better off than most people and there is no reason why, after you have worked as hard as you have and have been as successful as you have, you should not be willing to accept a reward by resting and spending some money on yourself, a thing which I have rarely ever seen you do. I know that, even if you don't think it would make you any happier to do this, that it would make me a lot happier to know that you were doing it. I hope this letter doesn't sound too childish and that it will not be in vain, but that it will be of some influence to you because after all it is far better to be happy than wealthy. I hope I see you soon. Please do not bother to answer this letter.

With lots of love

Joe[16]

The melancholy tone of this letter must have been influenced by Sailer's knowledge of his father's seriously failing health. Sailer may have seen him again after writing this letter, but not for long; Dr. Sailer died at home of heart disease on the last day of 1928, at the age of sixty-one, after being sick for several weeks. Sailer's mother maintained their large townhouse at 1718 Spruce Street, where the Sailers had moved in 1916, as the family's home base until 1942. She never considered remarrying, and she never allowed her wedding ring to leave her finger for any reason for the rest of her life.

Although his parents were strong models of behavior for Sailer in his early years, he also was exposed to numerous aunts and uncles. Some of them led quiet, respectable lives as stockbrokers or just as gentlemen and ladies. Two of them, though, were particularly colorful and embodied the independent and adventuring streak that surfaced in the family from time to time.

Great-uncle Herbert Welsh, born in 1873, was the brother of Sailer's grandmother, Alice Welsh Strawbridge, and the son of John Welsh, who had been minister to England. Herbert was an accomplished painter, having studied art in Philadelphia and then in Paris under Bonnat. Later, he spent some time with the Sioux Indians, and thereafter devoted much of his life to fighting for the rights of Indians across the country, eventually becoming president of the Indian Rights Association. In 1890, he led a citizens' revolt against "boss rule" in Pennsylvania. Besides his propensity for upholding noble civic causes, Herbert was known for his preferred mode of transportation each summer from Philadelphia to his vacation place at Sunapee, New Hampshire—walking. Each year, until he turned seventy-nine, he walked the distance of more than four hundred miles. He died in June 1941, at the age of eighty-nine.[17]

Although his great-uncle was a colorful and admirable figure, Sailer probably spent more time with his mother's sister, Aunt Anne West Strawbridge, born in 1883, who was called simply "Aunt" by those in the younger generation. Though she had much of the physical beauty of Sailer's mother, Mary, she never married, and eventually found outlets for her restless energies in several fields—mountain climbing, painting, writing, and aviation. As a young woman of eighteen she scaled the Matterhorn in Switzerland, one of the first women to do so.[18] Later she published several novels, and, at the age of about fifty-three, in June of 1936, she made her first solo flight in an autogiro, a curious aircraft popular at that time that looked like a cross between an airplane and a helicopter.[19] She owned her own autogiro, which over the course of a few years was to be a factor in two unfortunate events in her life. In August 1935, after she had purchased her autogiro but had not yet learned to fly it, she hired pilots to take it up for test flights. One summer evening, two young men were bringing the craft in for a landing at its home field near Philadelphia when the landing gear evidently hit an overhead electrical wire and the autogiro crashed to the ground. The pilot was killed and the passenger seriously injured.[20] After this disastrous accident, relatives advised her to give up the idea of owning her own aircraft, if only to keep from "killing people," as her brother Jack bluntly put it.[21] But she was not to be denied her avenues to adventure and independence, and went on to fly solo the next year, to the astonishment of some of her relatives. Joe Sailer wrote to his mother:

I got a letter from Aunt the other day and heard all about the big solo flight. It certainly surprised me, because I did not think that there was a chance that she would ever solo. You had better be the next to get an aeroplane.[22]

In her later years, Miss Strawbridge became increasingly eccentric; she lived alone, but employed a man to do yard work and maintenance around the house. One of this man's tasks was to hold up the morning newspaper outside her downstairs window so she could read it through the glass and avoid contact with the unsanitary paper. When new telephone directories or other books were brought into her house, she had them baked in the oven for a time sufficient, in her mind, to kill whatever unwelcome bacteria were harbored in the pages. Despite her harmless oddities, she was a generous and warm aunt to Sailer and his siblings, and he must have admired the adventuring spirit that took her up the Matterhorn and up in the autogiro. This unusual craft, though, which fitted her nature in its eccentric but quite successful design, was to contribute to her undoing. She continued flying it until the summer of 1941, when she was fifty-eight. Then, while searching for a place to store the flying machine for the winter, she became ill, and walked to Abington Memorial Hospital, where she asked to be admitted. She died there three weeks later, on September 9, 1941.[23]

CHAPTER TWO
THE THIRTIES

THERE IS NO RECORD of Sailer's attempts, if any, to find a job in engineering right after he graduated from Princeton with honors in mechanical engineering in 1930. In any event, his love of flying continued to be a strong impulse. This desire to fly, coupled with the scarcity of civilian jobs in the early years of the Depression and perhaps with the influence of his late father's record in the Marine Corps, left Sailer with a choice that must have been easy for him: he joined the volunteer Marine Corps Reserve as a private first class. He enlisted through a new program designed to develop a pool of trained aviators who would remain on standby in the reserves until needed on active duty.

In June 1930, right after graduation, he started his flight training at the U.S. Naval Reserve Aviation Base at Curtiss–Wright Airport, Valley Stream, Long Island. He found this to be a "fine and cool place . . . surrounded on all sides by water."[1] Out of his lifetime habit of offhanded self-deprecation, he mentioned to his mother that half of the class would be dropped after the first two or three weeks, "so I may be up in Camden very soon now."[2] At this point he had not yet had any military training, only aircraft maintenance and a very little flying; he had "no idea when to salute and when not to."[3] Sailer provided a matter-of-fact description of his roommate, Zimmerman, who did not quite measure up to Sailer's code of conduct, since he tried "to get a big drag with the officers by doing things for them whenever he gets a chance."[4]

By early July, Sailer and two others had soloed, ahead of the rest of the class. As it turned out, only one or two would be dropped out. Sailer, who seldom said (or, at least, wrote) very critical things about his colleagues, still was not pleased with Zimmerman, who was "about the messiest boy I have ever seen, & as a result I have gotten much neater than usual" in a fruitless attempt to influence Zimmerman for the better.[5] The flight instruction passed by quickly, and in mid-July of 1930 the class of volunteer reservists was off to the naval air station at Pensacola, in the western part of the Florida Panhandle, for nearly a year of a more thoroughly military approach to aviation. The one drawback to going south immediately was that Sailer would not be able to get to Camden that summer.

At Pensacola, as a Reserve Student Officer, Sailer was one of forty students to begin training in flying several types of airplanes, including pursuit planes (Vought O2U Corsairs) and "Hawk" fighters (probably Curtiss F6Cs), and learning the arts of navigation, radio communication, and aerial tactics and maneuvers, including bombing, gunnery, dogfighting, aerobatics, precision landings, and formation flying. He seemed to have no problem mastering the required skills; after his thirty-hour solo check he reported matter-of-factly to his mother that he had to be able to do "tail spins, flipper turns, flipper spirals and all sorts of emergency landings."[6] He then described the next milestone he would face on the next good flying day, a "boat shot," which involved

> climbing to 6,000 feet altitude, then comeing down to 3,000 feet in any manner at all. At 3,000 ft. you shut off your motor & spiral down to a landing which must be within 200 ft. of a buoy. It sounds sort of complicated but it is really very easy as only one boy has failed to make it on his first try so far.[7]

One of his letters to his mother during this period contains a reference to events that were occupying the Marines elsewhere. He reported that his friend Bill Carroll had come down with a mild form of malaria that apparently had been brought back by Marines serving in Nicaragua, where they had been fighting since 1926 (and engaging in some of the earliest Marine combat aviation) to protect United States interests that were jeopardized by that country's turbulent political situation.[8]

There was a lot of flying and studying, but plenty of time for golf; Sailer played as much as twenty-seven holes in a given day, and went to tournaments featuring some of the top players of the day. He also spent time at the beach, bowling, playing pool, dating, going to the movies, and participating in a craze that was fashionable at the time— dance marathons.

Sailer was quite a diligent correspondent when he had the time; his letters often express a rueful sense of guilt at letting a stack of letters from the family go unanswered for a time. In one letter to his sister Mary, he described how he had finally eased the burden of one neglected duty:

I have just taken a great load off my mind as I can still taste the glue off the envelope which I have finished sealing & which is addressed to Aunt Nancy [his father's sister]. She sent me a most wonderful cake which must have come nearly a month ago and I blush to admit that I have not written to her until now. I blundered thru the most mixed up letter that you can imagine in trying to thank her and she will probably be mader than if I hadn't written at all.[9]

One thing that is rarely found in any of his letters is any serious complaint, perhaps because most of the surviving letters are to his mother, whom he did not want to alarm. He often adopts an air of resigned self-criticism: "I have gotten in a lot of tennis but my game stays as poor as ever."[10] During this period, though, Sailer recorded some of his more private thoughts in what evidently was his only experiment in keeping a diary. He bought himself a pocket diary on February 14, 1931, while looking for a valentine for a girlfriend, and kept it up quite steadily until early June. In these entries, he occasionally describes minor setbacks and hardships, such as the time he got airsick over the side of the plane during training in very bumpy air.[11] During a phase of training that involved a lot of radio communication, he had a steady run of bad luck in getting radios that worked. In one diary entry he recorded the frustration and physical hardships in a matter-of-fact way:

Started radio to-day flying only in the morning 3 hrs. all together. Heist was the pilot & I the operator for the first hour & 1/2. I couldn't make the set work & finally had to put it on my lap getting several shocks from the generator. At the end of an hour I finally got it fixed & was in communication for 1/2. hour. Heist did very well as operator & received congratulations when he got down.[12]

After several more days of struggling with bad radios, Sailer reported to his diary:

Continued to have trouble with radio's. Heist operator first hr. & got 2 different sets but couldn't transmit. They changed planes for us & I got set no. 4 again. For the first time in 3 days I got radiation but they couldn't hear me on the ground. Changed to an M. B-1 set but couldn't hear on that either. No luck. Class all did poorly so they are going to hold us over for spotting.[13]

Nothing he encountered ever seemed to faze Sailer; he took it all in stride and kept on plugging away at his training and at packing his evenings and weekends with dates, movies, chess games, and, occasionally, reading books such as *Anna Karenina*.

The Pensacola flight training finished up at the end of April of 1931. Sailer had successfully completed his training in structure, power plant, gunnery, communications, seaplanes, land planes, observation planes, instrument flying, and "fighting" planes. He received his commission as a second lieutenant in the Marine Corps Reserve on May 20, 1931, and his naval aviator certificate on July 2, 1931. He headed up to Philadelphia on leave for a while, where he tried to persuade Pen, who was then eighteen, to join him in Camden. Sailer's letters often show his concern about his youngest brother, who seemed to suffer from the chronic problem of having "nothing to do."[14]

Sailer then headed up to Maine, where he was able to enjoy for a few weeks the normal summer routine of playing bridge, sailing, going to the lake in the afternoons, climbing Mount Battie, and spending time with his mother, siblings, and cousins. At the end of June, he went by train to San Diego for the next phase of his aviation training and his required year of active duty. On the trip west, Sailer especially enjoyed the scenery between Colorado and California, where the terrain was so "hilly and changing" that he sat out on the platform of the last car and watched it go by. On the final leg, from Los Angeles to San Diego, Sailer was the only passenger. Because he had a Pullman ticket, the railroad had to take his Pullman car all the way down. Sailer sat in the men's lounge with the conductor during the whole trip south and discussed the situation.[15]

Once in San Diego, Sailer and two Marine buddies named Peterson and Paul Brunk found a house in Coronado with two bedrooms, bathroom, library, dining room, and kitchen (with an "ice ice-box") for $55 a month. Sailer wasted no time in finding transportation in the form of a new black Ford roadster with red wheels, which he bought for $617.[16] Another early priority was to join the golf club. The days of ground school and flying ended by about 3:30, so there was plenty of time for recreation: golf, bridge, chess, photography, aquaplaning, swimming, trips to Mexico for beers in Tijuana and swimming at Rosereta Beach, and lots of dates. For one stretch he played golf from 4:00 to 5:30 every afternoon. He stayed in touch with home some nights by listening to the Philadelphia Athletics' baseball games on the radio, and took advantage of an opportunity to see the famous Australian horse Phar Lap win a race at the Agua Caliente Jockey Club in Mexico.[17] As he did several times over the years from different locations, he encouraged his mother to come out for a visit, although there is no indication that she ever did.

His letters draw the picture of a carefree year. In October, he wrote his mother about an "amusing time" he and his roommates had with two "girls," Emmy Spalding and Bobby Davis, who came over to the house to cook supper for Sailer and his roommates:

> Mrs. Spalding persuaded Emmy to cook the popovers & their cook supplied her with all the pots & pans necessary to make them. Severson [a replacement for Brunk, who got married] & I were both quite impressed when we saw them come barging into the kitchen with aprons & all their cooking utensils. We both took showers & shaved while they were cooking and emerged into the dining room feeling fresh & hungry only to find that the pop-overs didn't pop and that they had let all the water boil out of [the] peas and that they had burnt to the bottom of the pan. We had a great time kidding them about it & said that we could easily see why all the newly married reserves looked so undernourished for the first three or four weeks.[18]

Along with the fun and games, the flight training went on. Despite his unflappability, Sailer allowed some irritation to show in his diary entries about one instructor,

Larkin, who was "9 months from Pensacola" and a "pain in the neck." On one check flight, after Sailer and Larkin had gotten in the airplane, the instructor said, "What was the big idea in doing that?" When Sailer asked him "what?" Larkin replied, "So you don't even know what you did."[19] The next day, Larkin accused Sailer of having dived at 130 knots and not leveled off until 300 feet above the ground. The actual facts, as Sailer assured his diary: "Dove at 120 to stay out of clouds & leveled out at 800 ft. Typical of Larkin."[20]

By the beginning of 1932, the courses in law, Navy regulations, radio, and the like had about ended, and Sailer got to fly just about every good day. He got an introduction to dive-bombing, in maneuvers in which he took up six bombs, and dove from 3,000 to 2,000 feet, aiming at a ground target and dropping a single practice bomb filled with sand. He also practiced fixed gunnery and dogfighting through camera gunnery, in which each plane was equipped with a camera that took pictures of the targeted planes, allowing scoring of "hits" after the training session.[21] On the ground, he spent a week on the Marine Corps rifle range learning to shoot a rifle and pistol, but won only Sharpshooter medals, rather than Expert, much to his chagrin: "They are very nice looking medals but are really a big disgrace as all officers should get expert medals."[22]

As always, Sailer took advantage of the social opportunities in the area when work was not too pressing. He visited the racetrack at Agua Caliente on more than one occasion, not just to see Phar Lap, but to bet on the less well-known horses and generally enjoy the spectacle. On January 15, 1932, he attended an open golf tournament at the Agua

Caliente Golf and Country Club, where the field included Ben Hogan, Walter Hagan, Gene Sarazen, and many other luminaries of that era of professional golf. The first prize was $5,000 out of a $15,000 purse. One weekend in April he and Severson drove to Los Angeles with the plan of calling on everyone there that they knew. After an awkward and abortive attempt to visit an aunt of Sailer's brother-in-law, they ended up spending the night at the luxurious house of a movie director they had met earlier in Ensenada, and had a "wonderful time."[23] His brother John visited in June, and quickly entered into the California way of life, spending a lot of time sunning himself on the beach during the day and "stepping around" with the local girls at night.[24]

Meanwhile, the clock was ticking on his year of active duty, and it was time to think about life on the outside. Staying in the Marine Corps was not an option for those like Sailer who had joined the Reserves in this era. The master plan was to get good men trained as pilots, then "push them out," so that others could be trained. After the training and one year of active duty, the new aviators were to leave the active service and maintain their flying proficiency through weekend training.[25]

The job market in the civilian world looked very bleak. Sailer's dream throughout the pre-war years, at least until he eventually landed a steady job, was to become an airline pilot. To that end, in April 1932 he secured his civilian Transport Pilot's license, which allowed him to carry passengers for hire. But jobs of any kind, let alone pilots' positions, were very hard to come by, and employment with an airline was not in the cards at this point. Sailer and his housemates Ralston and Severson had animated discussions about the possibilities. They had resolved not to take office jobs, and considered the alternatives: prospecting for gold, buying a plane and barnstorming, or some other "wild & crazy adventure."[26]

To his credit, Sailer made good on this pledge. Although a number of his relatives, cushioned by family affluence that largely survived the Depression, had opted for comfortable, predictable lives as stockbrokers, lawyers, or gentleman farmers, there is no indication that Sailer ever considered this path of slight resistance. After completing his tour at San Diego, he dove decisively off the secure platform of military service and found himself in the desert at Chloride, Arizona, working for his sister Alice's husband's brother-in-law, Tom Denton, in a gold mine that offered plenty of hard work but precious little gold. Even in his letter congratulating his sister Mary on her engagement, Sailer allowed the frustrations of this life to poke through: "This mine is getting to be one of the most agonizing affairs that you have ever seen. As yet no ore has been found that amounts to a row of pins and every day Tom and I are looseing all the money we have."[27] He was soon "fed up" and headed home in December 1932, having stuck it out for the last six months of the year.

Sailer now was faced with the full impact of the Depression, and his options were limited. Although he probably could have survived on the family's resources, he was by no means content to do so, and he sent out letters following up on whatever leads he could muster to find a job related to engineering. For the first half of 1933 he found a job as a garage mechanic with the Doylestown & Easton Motorcoach Company in Philadelphia. Eventually, Sailer evidently concluded that it made more sense to improve his resume than to flounder in a stagnant job market. He decided on a change of scenery and headed for California in December 1933. He enrolled in the Boeing School of Aeronautics in Oakland, a division of United Air Lines, as a potential stepping-stone to a career as an airline pilot. Somewhat ironically, his method of traveling west was not by air, but on a Panama Pacific Line ship from New York to San Francisco by way of the Panama Canal, with stops in Havana, San Diego, and Los Angeles. Perhaps because of his new abilities as a leader of people, Sailer was put in charge of the ship's shuffleboard tournament and thereby "got to know practically every tourist passenger on the boat as it was a terrible job to get them together to play off their matches."[28]

Early 1934 saw him settled contentedly into a boarding house, having bought himself a new Ford. He got in about three hours a month of flying in the Reserves. He found companions for swimming and golf, and toured around in the new car on weekends. On one occasion, he heard of a wonderful restaurant with a waterfall, stream, and trees inside, but, upon arriving and finding that you had to buy fifty cents worth of food to get in, and having already eaten, he opted for frugality and passed up the opportunity.[29]

In the midst of this carefree way of life, though, Sailer was faced with one catastrophic event that tested his unflappable nature. In July 1934, while he was in the midst of a letter-writing campaign to find permanent employment, he went to stay for a few days at the home of Mrs. Chase, whose family he was friendly with. She had asked him to stay there because her husband was away on business and she did not want to be alone in the house. Her

31

daughter Frances, a good friend of Sailer's, was away on a camping trip to Lake Tahoe with her sister Margaret and another young woman. Sailer and Mrs. Chase were going to drive up there to meet them. But on July 18 at three in the morning the telephone rang. It was Margaret, reporting that she and her two companions had been in an automobile accident. As they were coming back from a dance in a car driven by a young man, the driver was unable to negotiate a turn, and the car went over a steep hill, hit a boulder, and finally stopped against a tree. The four riders were thrown out of the car; Frances Chase and her friend hit their heads on rocks and were killed instantly. Sailer spent much of the week making the funeral arrangements. In his letters he rarely revealed any emotion when writing about troubles or problems, taking the ups and downs of unemployment, hard work, annoying flight instructors, or daily inconveniences in stride. On this occasion, though, he showed some of his reaction in a letter to his mother, allowing that "[t]his last week has been simply terrible" and acknowledging that Frances' death "was really a terrible blow to me."[30]

He was diligent in his pursuit of jobs, but as of July 1934 he had written twelve letters to potential employers and received four responses, all of them "very discouraging."[31] He graduated from the Boeing school in July as a Master Mechanic, and, there being no prospects of a permanent job in aviation, went back East to spend some time working with a friend named Herbert Freuler on the design of an internal combustion engine. Sailer and Freuler eventually applied for a patent in 1935, but it evidently was denied by the Patent Office in 1936.[32] During the 1934–35 academic year, Sailer enrolled at the University of

Pennsylvania in Philadelphia to pursue a Master's degree in mechanical engineering, which he received in June 1935. Then, at last, after attempts with companies such as Pratt & Whitney, he landed full-time employment with United Air Lines as a ground agent in Fresno, California.

By September, he had been transferred to Medford, Oregon, a pleasant, mountainous area, which he found to be very appealing. He liked the idea that many people in the area owned gold mines, and reported that "I am all set to buy a little mine myself now when I can find one and go out and pan gold on my day off."[33] However, there was less work to do here than in Fresno, in part because of the frequent fogs, which kept planes from landing at his airport for days at a time. He kept up with his social life, golf, and handball, and thrived on the life in his boardinghouse. He had the opportunity to do some flying in a Monocoupe and a Taylor Cub, in which he logged a total of about eight hours from January to March. He earned forty cents an hour with United, and enjoyed the work. He kept a careful watch on his health, and enthusiastically embraced what he saw as the latest panacea in the field of medicine:

> I have been walking around some of the hills around here and picked up a slight case of poison ivy, so immediately went down to the doctor to get innoculated, and now it has practically all dried up. In the future I am going to get innoculated for everything that you can be innoculated for, because it certainly works wonders for me. I have never in my life seen so many people who have colds and the grip as everyone seems to

have in Medford. Once or twice I could feel a cold coming on, and in each case I would go to the doctor and get another innoculation and in less than a day would be in perfect health again.[34]

Towards the end of his brief stay in Oregon, he encountered another in a series of accidents he would witness throughout his life, and he characteristically plunged coolly into the middle of it, taking efficient steps to deal with disaster without a second thought:

> About a month ago I had quite an exciting experience. I was driving out to the airport at 11:30 pm, and in front of me there was a small delivery truck, which later turned out to be a delivery truck for a meat concern in Medford. I must have been about 200 ft. behind the truck, when as we were going around a bend in the road I could see a car coming in the opposite direction. Just as this car was about to pass the truck for some unknown reason it pulled over to the wrong side of the road and the two cars hit head on. Immediately there was a burst of flames. The car that had run into the truck was an Austin and the whole front of it had been completely smashed in. The flames were so bright that it lit everything up just like daylight, and in the Austin was a man and a girl who were all slumped over. I ran up and tried to pull the man out before the flames got back to him, but I could not get him out because his feet were caught in the front of the car that had all been pushed back. After struggling with him for about a minute I could see that I was

not making any headway and ran around to the other side of the car to see if I could get the girl out. Her feet were also caught, but I finally got them free, and when I lifted her out of the car, her right leg was so badly fractured that it looked as if it were made out of rubber from the knee to the ankle. By this time some other cars had stopped and three men were trying to get the man out. I laid the girl on the side of the road far enough away so that she would not catch on fire and then ran to call up the ambulance and fire department.[35]

In July 1936, he was transferred back much closer to home, and worked for United at the Camden, New Jersey, airport, living at home in Philadelphia, just across the Delaware River.

However, another opportunity was soon to intervene. Sailer had received his promotion to first lieutenant in the reserves in the summer of 1936, and, early in 1937, the Marine Corps offered him a chance to return to active duty for fifteen months. He asked United for a leave of absence from his position as passenger agent, stating that "this is an opportunity which may not present itself again" and that the additional service "would give me a chance to do considerable flying and learn the most recent developments in navigation," helping him to qualify as a copilot for United in the future.[36] The leave of absence was granted in a cordial letter that deemed his work to date "very satisfactory," though there was no absolute guarantee of re-employment upon his return.[37]

He reported in April to the Marine Barracks at Quantico, Virginia, where he was assigned to Aircraft One, First

Marine Brigade. He moved in with his old Marine buddy from San Diego, Martin Severson, who was scheduled to leave soon for a posting in the Virgin Islands. Sailer found that the "officers as usual are treated like kings with very elegant quarters."[38]

During this period he was able to continue with much of his normal social life, since his Philadelphia relatives and friends were only a short train ride away. He stayed in touch with his brother John, who had finished law school and was approaching the point of marrying his steady girl-friend. John kept up a friendly course of comment on Joe's marriage prospects, encouraging Joe to settle down with his hottest flame of the moment, a young woman named Ledlie Newlin from Bryn Mawr, a fashionable suburb on Philadel-phia's Main Line. By June of 1937, though, the romance with Ledlie had foundered, and Joe's future sister-in-law, Marion Crozer, wrote Joe that she was "so disappointed that we are not going to have a double announcement."[39] Joe evidently never paused for long in lining up dates, and by late June was seeing a young woman from Washington, D.C.

By the end of June he was transferred to Pensacola as a flight instructor. He soon took to instructing, and, drawing on his summer experience in Camden over the years, plunged into a full schedule of sailing on the side. He set up regattas and other races as chairman of the yacht club's sailboat committee, and, eventually, as the sailing officer for the base. One of his fellow instructors, Horace Mazet, who years later was to write an article about Sailer's service at Guadalcanal, remembered him as a man of contrasts:

> Joe was sometimes smiling and sometimes grim. Unpredictable. . . . I recall that one day I slid a

firecracker down the corridor to his open door
and it went off; he came storming out and was
ready to trade blows, mad as hell, but eventually
he cooled off and nothing was further made of
the caper. (Others I had treated likewise with no
untoward reactions.)[40]

He was promoted to captain in early 1938, with a raise
in pay from $290 to $345 a month. This promotion gave his
brother John an idea for what he thought was a fine and
mischievous practical joke. John sent Joe a realistic, but
fake telegram at the naval air station, saying:

OVERJOYED ABOUT YOUR ELEVATION TO
RANK OF CAPTAIN UNDERSTAND EXAMI-
NATION IS MERE FORMALITY PITY TO LOSE
EXTRA COMPENSATION AWARDED MAR-
RIED OFFICERS MY LOVE UNABATED IF
YOUR FEELING UNCHANGED WHY NOT
JOIN ON BUSINESS BASIS I WOULD BE WILL-
ING TO RELEASE YOU AT WILL GIVE THIS
SERIOUS CONSIDERATION
LOVE AND KISSES
LEDLIE

Joe was not amused, and so advised his brother in definite
terms. His chances of remaining in the service at this point
were not great, although he would have liked to stay in if
possible, and the telegram had been transmitted directly to
the naval air station, where the contents evidently leaked
rather quickly. Within a week, a contrite John wrote back,
apologizing for what he had thought was a "harmless joke."

Over the next few weeks, though, John and Joe corresponded about a new romance that was blooming for Joe in Pensacola, and they discussed the options that were open to him: try to stay with the Marines to be near her, or take her with him to settle down wherever he could find a civilian job. Even then it was apparent that Joe was thinking of the prospects of marriage in light of the disruptions of war. Although there is no letter of his that says so, it seems likely that the shadow of the coming war was one factor that kept him from ever settling down with anybody. In any event, he never married, and there is no indication that he was ever engaged, despite a fairly steady string of romantic attachments.

In advising his mother of the 1938 promotion and raise, Sailer noted that he was "investing everything I can spare in the stock market," though it "keeps going down." He remarked that he had his eye on three stocks, one of which, Sperry Gyroscope Company, Inc., he thought to be "particularly good" because the government would be building new military planes and ships, which "carry a lot of Sperry equipment."[41] This interest in Sperry had more important implications for Sailer's future than as an investment of unspent salary. By late 1938, it had become clear that the fifteen-month tour of active duty would not be extended indefinitely. In Sailer's delicate phraseology in a letter to Sperry, "[b]ecause of an over-supply of instructors here, the U.S. Marine Corps views favorably a desire to obtain other employment."[42] He had tried for a job with Pan American World Airways, but without success. This time around, he finally hit upon a company that suited his interests, and whose needs he could fulfill.

Facing a mandatory separation from active duty by the end of the year, and exploiting what contacts he could,

Sailer traveled to New York in early November 1938 and contacted a friend from the Marine Corps, James Webb, who, like Sailer, had joined the reserves in 1930 and taken his flight training at Pensacola. Webb, trained as a lawyer, already had made some important connections in politics and industry, and by 1936 had become director of personnel at Sperry, where he would eventually hold several high positions. He ultimately would be appointed administrator of the National Aeronautics and Space Administration by President Kennedy in 1961.[43] In 1938 Webb was willing and able to arrange an interview for his Pensacola colleague on short notice, and it bore fruit. Events moved quickly, and, by the first of December, Sailer had been detached from active duty, and was working for Sperry in Brooklyn, living in the St. George Hotel with Bill Harcum of Sperry; Sailer's lodging payment was about $10.00 a week. The Marine Corps assigned him to Marine Reserve Scouting Squadron Two, Naval Reserve Aviation Base, Floyd Bennett Field, Brooklyn.

CHAPTER THREE
SPERRY

When Joe Sailer first reported for work at Sperry's Brooklyn headquarters at the end of 1938, it seemed as if he had finally settled down. He was working in his chosen field of engineering, he got to continue his flying in the reserves, and he had good friends. One of his married colleagues, Franklin Joseph, invited him over for quite a few Sunday dinners with him and his wife, Eleanor. Franklin Joseph later recalled one telling characteristic that showed up during these dinners:

> Joe had one harmless idiosyncrasy that may shed light on his organized mind. When served dinner, he would finish one item on the plate before going on to the second item. I recall his eating all the peas and my wife giving him a second portion right away. Joe, with his self-imposed restrictions, felt obligated to finish the second portion before selecting the second item on the plate.[1]

He continued to see a variety of women, including one, a psychiatric nurse named Hilma Newman, who later said she would always remember the "awfully good times" she and Joe had spent together during this period.[2] He enjoyed corresponding with his nephew, Bill White, who was about to turn five years old. Sailer always had deep affection for his sister Mary, and he and Mary's son carried on quite a correspondence as Bill began to learn how to write. Sailer asked him how he was getting along with his Erector Set, and invited him up to see the New York World's Fair. Sailer also saw his sister Alice at the World's Fair, with her husband, Lawrence Litchfield, who by this time was the president of a subsidiary of the Aluminum Company of America (Alcoa). Sailer kept up with the Litchfields at other times by dropping in on them at their home in New Canaan, Connecticut, where he played with the children, once trying on the child-sized skis of his niece Mary, and dissolving in a fit of his infectious laughter after he collapsed in the snow. And, to the displeasure of his military superiors, more of his playful nature emerged when on at least one occasion he buzzed the Litchfields' house in a plane he was flying on reserve duty. He still could show his stern and proper side; once, when his young niece Priscilla said something negative about public schools, her uncle admonished her never to say such a thing, because some of the finest and most successful people in the country had gone to public schools.[3]

It was also during this period, in late 1939 or the summer of 1940, that one particular incident brought together Sailer's work at Sperry with his aviation background, and illustrated once more his ability to maintain his calm demeanor in the face of sudden crisis. His Sperry colleague Carl Frische described what happened:

I will never forget this episode. It is not so much what Joe did, but how he went about it. Joe and I were out at Floyd Bennett Field in Brooklyn doing something in the new Sperry Flight Research airplane. . . . We were probably making a bomb sight installation. Our airplane was parked in front of the open door of the hangar along side of Jackie Cochran's single engine biplane. A mechanic was working on the engine, all alone and climbed into the cockpit to start the engine without standing fire guard. No sooner had the engine started with a roar when the space under the engine and the front of the airplane erupted in flame fanned into a blowtorch by the propeller. Joe went into the hangar, picked up a big fire extinguisher, walked up to the spinning propeller and put out the fire. It was as though he did this every morning before breakfast. He returned the fire extinguisher into the hangar where it belonged and came back to work with me without saying a word. I don't think that Jackie's mechanic ever knew that he was almost burned to a crisp.[4]

The primary focus of Sailer's time in Brooklyn and at Sperry, though, was his engineering work. As he had perceived while still on active duty in the Marine Corps, Sperry was well-situated to make a significant contribution to the increasing preparations for war. The company designed and manufactured a variety of control systems with military applications, most of them based on the device that figured prominently in the company's name—the gyroscope.

As anyone who has come in contact with science toys is aware, a gyroscope is a wheel that can spin very rapidly within a framework that allows the wheel to maintain its stability even when the framework is tilted in any direction. This principle has been applied in various devices, including the gyrocompass, which, once aligned, always points to true north without the need for magnetic attraction; in anti-roll equipment on ships; in torpedo guidance systems; in aircraft autopilots; and in bomb sights.[5] The first gyrocompass made in the United States was invented by Elmer Ambrose Sperry (1860–1930), who had earlier invented a wide range of electrical machines for various industrial applications.[6] In 1910 he founded the Sperry Gyroscope Company, Inc., in Brooklyn. The company, which eventually went on through mergers to fields such as farm machinery and computers (most recently as part of Unisys Corporation), originally concentrated on using the gyroscope principle in compasses and other guidance equipment for aircraft and ships. Two devices had critical importance for the military, and became extremely important parts of Joe Sailer's professional life: the autopilot and the bomb sight.

In simple terms, an autopilot mechanism uses the gyroscopic principle to stabilize an aircraft by keeping the wings level and the craft headed in the proper direction. A bomb sight is considerably more complex: it is a device that enables a bombardier aboard an airplane to drop bombs at the precise moment that will cause them to hit the intended target with precision, based on many variables, including the airplane's speed, altitude, and heading, as well as the temperature, barometric pressure, wind direction and velocity, type of bomb, and other factors.[7] Although a bomb sight theoretically could handle these calculations independent of the aircraft's controls if the plane were maintained on a known, steady course and speed, to work effectively and with the required precision in actual practice it was necessary to connect the bomb sight to an autopilot.[8] Thus, during the bombing procedure, the bomb sight would actually control the plane's flight while the device calculated the exact moment for the bomb release.

The Sperry company first started working on bomb sights in 1914, when one of its employees was Carl Norden. That engineer's name later became associated with the more famous Norden bomb sight, which he developed after he left Sperry. By 1933, Sperry had developed its own model O-1 bomb sight. In 1937, Dr. Carl A. Frische, a Sperry physicist who worked closely with Sailer and taught him how to operate the bomb sight, together with O.E. Esval, installed a new type of gyroscope into the sight, greatly improving its performance.[9] After testing the new configuration, Dr. Frische's engineering group realized that the bomb sight would have to be mated to an autopilot mechanism to be really effective. They rigged it up to work with the Sperry A-3 autopilot. In 1939, Sailer, who had become an expert in the operation of the O-1, conducted in-house training classes at Sperry on the theory and operation of the O-1 sight.[10] However, there was competition from the Norden bomb sight, and a need to improve the Sperry equipment constantly. As a consequence, the O-1 bomb sight soon became obsolete.

The war had started in Europe and, by mid-1940, England was under siege in the Battle of Britain. Its destroyer force had suffered considerable losses in early naval conflicts and the evacuation at Dunkirk. After consideration of several proposals to assist the British, President Roosevelt proposed to transfer fifty aging destroyers to Britain in exchange for ninety-nine-year leases on military bases in the Bahamas, Jamaica, Antigua, St. Lucia, Trinidad, and British Guiana. By August the arrangements had been made, and transfer of the destroyers began at Halifax, Nova Scotia, where British, Canadian, and other allied crews prepared to sail them back to England. The destroyers were re-named from their United States Navy designations to names chosen from a list of British and American towns with the same names. This group of ships thus became known informally as the "town class destroyers," and they made significant contributions to the war effort, particularly in anti-submarine activities.[11]

Although the formal Lend Lease arrangement was not to be enacted by Congress until 1941, President Roosevelt made available to the British certain armaments and other valuable military equipment in 1940. Among the items sent over along with the vintage destroyers were twenty B-17 bombers, a large number of Lockheed Hudson twin-engined bombers, and forty Sperry O-1 bomb sights, which, although being supplanted by an improved model, still could be of considerable use to the Royal Air Force in precision bombing over Germany and other hostile areas.[12]

By the summer of 1940, many events were coming to a head that would affect Sailer's military and engineering careers. The country was in a Limited National Emergency as war approached, and in October he wrote his mother that "there has certainly been a lot of commotion during the past week about mobilizing the reserves." It looked as if his reserve unit in Brooklyn would be "mobilized in about a month or so."[13] Shortly before that, in September, Sailer had formally applied for a commission in the regular Marine Corps. However, Sperry at the same time needed to send some representatives to England to instruct British bomber pilots and other personnel in the operation and maintenance of the forty O-1 bomb sights that were being sent over. At this time, the existence of such devices was a closely guarded military secret; the company never even admitted during this period that it made bomb sights.[14] Sailer gave some veiled hints of what was in the wind, though; he told his mother that "something of a very confidential nature has come up at Sperry & there is some talk about sending me to England if I want to go."[15] He did, and one of his two major missions of the war was under way.

Although Sailer and the other Sperry employees who were sent to England were sent as civilian representatives of the company,[16] Sailer was still a member of the Marine Corps Reserve. Thus, in his case, the Marine Corps was involved in the arrangements for the trip. On October 17, 1940, Sailer received orders authorizing him to travel overseas for five months and deferring his mobilization, which had been imminent. The orders noted that this procedure would not interfere with his pending request for a commission in the regular corps, but, for the time being, he remained in the reserves.

Sailer was an ideal choice for the mission to England: a seasoned military aviator with experience in bombing techniques, an engineer who knew enough about the bomb sight and autopilot to teach courses on them at Sperry, and a man who had a wonderful gift of getting along with people. He also was considered absolutely reliable. One of his mentors, Carl Frische, later would say: "Those of us who worked with Joe in those days remarked that if he was ordered by his commanding officer to march straight into a spinning airplane propeller that Joe would salute and promptly do so."[17]

On Tuesday, October 22, 1940, a chartered American Airlines DC-3 was brought into a hangar at La Guardia Airport in New York. A Sperry truck was driven into the hangar, and, behind closed doors, the airplane was loaded with large wooden boxes containing the first shipment of O-1 bomb sights to be sent to the British. Sailer's partner on the mission overseas was Frederic Blin Vose, a 1922 graduate of the Naval Academy and Sperry's aeronautical sales manager. The DC-3 flew Sailer, Fred Vose, and the bomb sights to Ottawa, in Ontario, Canada. They spent some time there and in Halifax, Nova Scotia, over the next few days, meeting with Canadian air force and British navy officers, making preparations for the trip to England. Eventually, the crates of bomb sights were transferred to a Canadian air force Lockheed Hudson bomber, and Group Captain Pearce of the British RAF flew the Americans and the equipment to Halifax. There they rendezvoused with a convoy including three of the "flush deck" destroyers that were being sent to England on October 31 as part of the "destroyers-for-bases" deal.

During this period, the Battle of the Atlantic was in full operation; German U-boats were preying on merchant shipping carrying supplies to Britain, which was heavily dependent on the goods transported across the ocean. After July 1940, when the Germans got control of ports in occupied France and Norway, the U-boats expanded their area of operation. Thus, in October 1940, when Sailer and Vose embarked in the convoy for England, the marauding submarines were sinking British, allied, and neutral shipping at a rate of about 400,000 tons per month.[18] Because of this considerable threat of a submarine torpedo attack, Sailer and Vose traveled on separate ships. Sailer traveled on HMS *Lincoln*, a 314-foot destroyer with a top speed of 28.75 knots that had been commissioned in the U.S. Navy in 1918 as USS *Yarnall*.[19] He and Vose divided the bomb sights between the two ships as well, storing them securely in the destroyers' warhead magazines to increase the chances of getting at least one set of the devices to England in the event of an attack on the convoy. Despite the secrecy, the delivery of the bomb sights received substantial press coverage. Sailer couldn't give his mother any details, but in his letter to her from Halifax just before sailing for England, he gave a hint: "Maybe you have seen some of the news in the papers as it has been in both the N.Y. and Canadian papers."[20] *The New York Times* of October 26, 1940, reported, in a headline on page 4: "BOMB SIGHT REPORTED RELEASED TO BRITISH."

On the first night of the convoy's voyage, the going was rough, and, according to Sailer, most of the men on board HMS *Lincoln* got seasick. He, however, "felt well the whole time, ate all meals & slept like a top."[21] Coming into St. John's, Newfoundland, on the morning of November 2, Sailer reported that the travelers were presented with a "beautiful sight." It is not clear what that sight was, but presumably it involved an assemblage of ships or other military equipment, because about the next two inches in the middle of his letter were neatly scissored out by the Canadian military censor.[22] He had some time for shopping and sightseeing in St. John's before the convoy resumed its journey the next morning. Although neither Sailer's nor Vose's ship was attacked by the Germans, both were involved in action at sea. Towards the end of the crossing, HMS *Lincoln* left the convoy to rescue the survivors of a ship that had been bombed; ultimately thirty-four of the forty-two men from that ship were saved. Meanwhile, on Vose's ship, a depth charge rolled off the stern accidentally and exploded, creating a very creditable facsimile of hostile bombing.

The convoy survived without further incident, and arrived at Belfast, Northern Ireland, on November 11.[23] Sailer and Vose made their way by air to Farnborough, about thirty-two miles outside of London, the site of an RAF installation. In flying and driving through England in the first days after his arrival, Sailer was amazed at the relatively minimal damage he could see after the terrible bombardments of the Battle of Britain. In Farnborough, he was shown "two places where bombs had landed but the destruction was negligible & the holes filled up."[24] A few days later, on a trip to London, he did see for the first time "real damage." The people he saw looked "very tired and pale" and "the destruction in places is terrible although in other parts it is not noticeable." He went on to give his impressions of the English reaction to the bombardments:

> Everywhere, even if the houses themselves are not blown, you see windows which have been blown out by the explosions. It is, however, full of people & life, in the daytime, is perfectly normal, buses, taxies, automobiles, & everything just as you would expect if there had been no bombing. That evening the siren blew & nobody seemed to pay any attention to it, even though you could hear the German planes flying over, and there was lots of gunfire. At eight-thirty when it was very dark with lots of noise we got a taxi & went

to a restaurant and there were people every-
where. We left that evening at about eleven &
drove back to Farnborough but there was no aerial activity because of rain.

About every evening we hear German planes
flying over & sometimes the anti-aircraft fire but
there are no raids here & we feel just as safe as if
we were in New York.

There is one thing of which I am absolutely
convinced & that is the absolute truthfulness of all
the reports written by the English. The air raids by
day have absolutely stopped because the Germans
were loosing so many planes and at night the
accuracy is poor excepting on very big targets.[25]

Armed with a generous letter of credit from Sperry,[26]
Sailer settled in to a very comfortable room at the Queen's
Hotel in South Farnborough. The hotel was equipped with
a fine bomb shelter of concrete under six feet of earth. The
food was excellent, and the British extended every courtesy and convenience in the way of transportation and
entertainment. For local trips, Sailer had a bicycle with
three forward speeds, unusual at that time. Between riding
the bike every day and walking up to six miles some days,
he felt very fit and healthy. In his spare time, he went on
tours of the countryside and shopped for clothes and old
silver in the fine shops of London.[27] By January, Fred Vose
had returned to the United States and Sailer had moved to
Boscombe Down, where the British set him up with a
"simply magnificent room with fireplace and someone to
keep it in wonderful order at all times."[28] In fact, he was
assigned a "batman," who brought a cup of tea first thing

each morning, drew hot water for baths, laid out fresh clothes, and shined Sailer's shoes every night. According to Franklin Joseph, Sailer occasionally would make sure to get some mud on his shoes just so the batman would have something to accomplish.[29]

He did, of course, have a great deal of work to do at the RAF installations at Farnborough and Boscombe Down. His primary responsibility was to instruct the RAF officers and technicians at both installations in the theory and operation of the Sperry O-1 bomb sight. He had a workshop set up in a former gatekeeper's house in Farnborough.[30] He installed equipment in planes that were turned over to the British, including Lockheed Hudson bombers. He visited RAF operational squadrons and talked to British bombardiers to learn of their actual problems under wartime conditions over Germany.[31] He spent a good deal of time with men such as Ivor Bowen, deputy director of armament research with the Ministry of Aircraft Production, and took a large quantity of moving and still pictures to analyze the bomb sights' performance.[32]

He and Vose were fascinated by much of what they saw. One aspect of the work going on at Farnborough was analyzing captured enemy aircraft. The Sperry team watched with great interest, and made color motion pictures, as the British took a largely undamaged twin-engine Messerschmitt 110 up for a test flight, accompanied by an Allied plane as escort, to avoid having the German plane shot down by mistake. The British and Americans were somewhat surprised to learn that the Messerschmitt, contrary to what they believed, was well-equipped with up-to-date armaments and was quite easy to fly.

The Americans were impressed with the camouflage with which the British had concealed the air base at

Boscombe Down from aerial view; they likened it to a "gigantic mirage,"[33] in which each building, airplane, roadway, and runway was painted with flat blacks, drabs, and greens. Well-concealed anti-aircraft emplacements were scattered about the field. As they took their test flights in Hudsons and other aircraft, sometimes as many as four flights a day, they occasionally were rewarded by flying over sights such as Stonehenge and the cathedral at Salisbury.

Eventually, after testing the bomb sight at medium altitudes in Hudsons, the Americans got an opportunity to test it at high altitude from a B-17 Flying Fortress, the first of those arriving from America under the ongoing military assistance program. At this stage in aviation history, flying at such levels—generally above 32,000 feet—was new and far from routine. Considerable preparation was involved in adapting the pilots and crew to the conditions at what were termed "sub-stratospheric" altitudes. Each man underwent training in a decompression chamber to prepare for the near-vacuum conditions that were present in the airplane. The crew members all wore electrically heated suits over heavy clothing, and were outfitted with oxygen tanks and parachutes. Just dressing for each flight was a lengthy process, perhaps more analogous to preparing for a modern mission into space than to taking a modern high-altitude airplane flight. On one flight in warm weather, the temperature varied from 115 degrees Fahrenheit in the cabin before takeoff to 67 degrees below zero at 35,000 feet, within the space of one hour. Despite the obstacles of high-altitude flight, the bomb sight operated well, and the preliminary tests were concluded satisfactorily.

In carrying out this mission, Sailer was serving at least three organizations: Sperry, the British government, and the United States government. The Marine Corps was by no means a passive observer. While he was in England, as the threat of war increased, he was transferred from the reserves to the regular Marine Corps, but not without complications. At first, the Marine Corps bureaucracy insisted that he return to the United States by February 1, 1941, as a condition of receiving a regular commission. Finally, however, after a blizzard of correspondence back and forth, the Marine Corps headquarters in Washington decided that he could receive his commission in London and remain in his present duties in England for a few more months.[34] His written orders ultimately provided that he was to report to the United States naval attache at the American embassy in London to be examined for his commission. The orders, dated January 7, 1941, stated: "In view of the importance of the project on which you are working, it is the intention of this office, if you are found qualified, to accomplish your appointment without your having to return to the United States at the present time. . . ." Accordingly, he reported to the naval attache and received his regular commission as of February 25, 1941. Shortly afterwards, on March 21, he received orders authorizing him to "fly in aircraft of the Royal Air Force, both locally and on operational flights, as a spectator or observer," but "not to take an operational part in any activity of the Royal Air Force. . . ."

In mid-April, as had been arranged, the Marine Corps was to bring Sailer, now on active duty in the regular Marine Corps, back to the United States as a flight instructor. Sperry issued Sailer a $1,000 bonus check for his contribution to the company's national defense program, and sent Franklin Joseph to England as his replacement. Sailer spent a week showing him the ropes, and taking him around to meet all the British personnel he would be working with. Franklin Joseph recalled one of his first nights in Farnborough, staying in twin beds in Sailer's hotel room:

It became very noisy at 4:30 this morning when a dozen H.E. [high-explosive] bombs were dropped through the hangars. . . . Joe and I awoke with the first explosion. We didn't talk for some time. We were well under the covers, and at each explosion we would dig down under, further toward the foot of the bed.[35]

On one other occasion during their overlapping week in England, Sailer and Joseph had an encounter with what for the British was now a rare delicacy. Franklin Joseph related the incident:

One time we were walking down Piccadilly on a Sunday afternoon when he [Sailer] spotted a street vendor selling oranges. In food-scarce war-time London, Joe hadn't seen an orange in six months. He handed me an orange with glee and selected one for himself before knowing the price was exorbitantly high, four or five times the normal price. But he dug in and took care of it with cheer.[36]

On April 25, Franklin Joseph accompanied Sailer on the train to Bristol, where Sailer was to catch a KLM Airlines DC-3 to Lisbon, and then travel in the Pan American World Airways Yankee Clipper to New York. At the Bristol airport they met the other passengers who would be on the flight to Lisbon with Sailer: Major General Henry "Hap" Arnold, the head of the United States Army Air Forces (and one of the co-founders of Pan American years before[37]), General Schanlin of the United States Embassy, Commander Dow of the United States Navy, and Thomas Campbell, who owned a wheat farm of 96,000 acres in Montana. The DC-3 had what General Arnold called "blinders" over the windows until they were 300 miles out of England.[38] Once they arrived in Lisbon, on April 27, there was a wait of about a week for the Pan American flight before Sailer finally made it back to the states and home.

At this time, the Pan American Clipper took over as the only way for a commercial passenger to travel across the Atlantic, and places on the great flying boat were coveted by the privileged few who could get them. Portugal had maintained neutrality while Hitler undertook his conquest of Europe, and many refugees from the devastation of the war made their way to Lisbon, either as a temporary haven or as the gateway to a more permanent sanctuary in America.[39] Sailer was not quite privileged enough to catch the first flight out; General Arnold, Mr. Campbell, and twenty-four other passengers embarked at Lisbon on a Clipper that left Lisbon on April 28 and arrived in New York on May 1; Sailer was left waiting in Lisbon for a few days after that, and ultimately made it to New York on May 9. The Clipper's route, as recounted six months later by Sailer's Sperry colleague, Franklin Joseph, was exotic and circuitous: from Lisbon to stops at Bolama, Portuguese Guinea; Natal, Brazil; Belem, Paraguay, on the Amazon; Port-au-Spain, Trinidad; and Bermuda, before finally touching down at La Guardia Airport in New York. The legs of the flight on the spacious, 106-foot-long Boeing 314 were as long as fourteen hours, during which the passengers could walk about freely, play bridge, and relax in quiet comfort, as the flight was directed by a crew of five men upstairs on the flight deck and the passengers' needs were catered to by four male pursers.[40] The passengers' area was covered with rich and colorful carpeting, and furnished with fine upholstered chairs. The dining room offered formal place settings of real silverware and china on linen-covered tables.[41] There were lengthy, leisurely stopovers and pleasant meals in scenic tropical settings; the description evokes the aura of an ocean crossing, with camaraderie and enjoyment of the trip, a phenomenon of the dawn of transatlantic commercial flight.[42]

In any event, the efforts of Sailer, Vose, Franklin Joseph, and their colleagues in England were successful; on April 30, 1941, when Sailer was en route back to the United States, the Sperry bomb sight was used in its first operational attack. Using a Lockheed Hudson Mark V bomber into which the sight had been installed under Sailer's supervision, the RAF, under special orders from the British Air Ministry, launched a daylight attack from its base at Dyce, Scotland. The crew trained in cooperation with Sailer and other Sperry officials at Boscombe Down. After the series of experimental trials, a flight crew led by Flight Lieutenant John Mallinson was directed to test the sight in combat in an attack on enemy shipping at Tyboron Harbor, Denmark. Because of the secrecy of the new bomb sight, they were given strict orders to prevent its falling into enemy hands; in the event of trouble, the aircraft was to be ditched in deep water. The mission was particularly difficult because of the distance to the target, which necessitated a six-hour flight.

The mission succeeded, though; flying at 8,000 feet, below the cloud base, the Hudson's crew used the Sperry equipment to zero in on its target, an armed German supply ship of 700 to 800 tons. With only one salvo, the bomber scored a direct hit on the stern of the vessel.[43] Carl A. Frische, the Sperry engineer who had invented the autopilot component of the bomb sight and was largely instrumental in developing the successful equipment, later commented that, because Sailer had left England just a few days before this bombing run took place, it was "quite obvious that the fine results obtained on this first mission must be attributed to Joe's good job as a teacher and maintenance expert."[44]

After this first successful combat test, the crew returned to Boscombe Down to plan for a test under night combat conditions. This test was carried out on May 17, 1941. On this occasion, the same crew took off from the RAF base at Thorney Island, on the south coast of England, and flew in full moonlight to its target, a Benz factory at Cherbourg, in occupied France. This particular target was chosen for the precision-bombing test because it was located near a hospital, and accuracy was especially important. Flying at 12,000 feet, the crew again was successful in hitting the objective.[45]

Although Sailer went on RAF flights to test equipment, train personnel, and observe conditions (he is seen in Sperry's 1942 in-house movie, "Experiences in England," operating the gun turret of a Lockheed Hudson bomber), he never went on an actual bombing run. His Sperry colleague Fred Vose eventually did get to go on a raid, in a successful RAF mission over Bremen, Germany, on September 2, 1941.[46] In doing so, Vose became the first American to make an operational trip in the Flying

Fortress and the first American to fly into Germany on a long-range daylight bombing raid.[47]

In his account written some time after the Sperry bombing runs of 1941, John Mallinson (later wing commander) gave this evaluation of the O-1 bomb sight:

> The Sperry 0-1 was, unquestionably the most accurate bombsight used by the RAF. Had it been available earlier it would have saved many aircraft during the low level anti-shipping attacks. These ships were carrying vital strategic materials needed by the enemy and the vessels were heavily armed. The Nordern [sic] bombsight was not available for the RAF and I cannot comment on its alleged accuracy. The United States entered the War in the [sic] December and the whole aspect of precision bombing altered.[48]

However, despite these initial successes with the new equipment, the British military did not follow up with sufficient investment of money and training to pursue the use of the Sperry sight for precision bombing. Major General Arnold after his fact-finding trip to England in May 1941 observed that the British were committed to night bombing, and would not use the daylight precision-bombing approach.[49] The Americans themselves did not make extensive use of the Sperry sight; it was used in squadrons of B-24E bombers of the 15th Air Force in Italy,[50] and it was used very successfully for precision bombing of an assembly plant at Bad Voslau, Austria, on April 12, 1944, and of the Hermann Goering Tank Works at Linz, Austria, on July 25, 1944.[51] However, as was noted by Wing Commander Mallinson, the Sperry sight was highly accurate when used properly. The decisions by the British and Americans not to use that device extensively were the result of a complex mixture of historical circumstances, personalities, and other considerations, and should not be considered as an accurate reflection of the inherent value of the equipment itself, which was considerable.[52]

CHAPTER FOUR
PREPARING FOR WAR

Back in the States, Sailer was assigned to Quantico with the First Marine Aircraft Group, in Squadron VMSB-131.[1] His life was not too pressured at first; he went on a three-day cruise on an aircraft carrier, and was called on to give a speech before 150 men on his experiences in England; he wrote his mother that he was "saved" by the Dale Carnegie course he had taken.[2] Later, he noticed a new recreational phenomenon that was becoming popular, and could not resist sharing it with the family up in Camden:

> At the swimming pool here a lot of the people are starting to wear rubber things that fit on your feet called Swim-Fins. You can swim much faster with them and they are lots of fun. I dont know if you have seen them or heard of them yet, but have ordered four pairs to be sent to you to try out in Maine.

He did indeed send the swim fins back home, and they were enjoyed by his nieces, nephews, and others at the lake in Maine for many years thereafter.

For the next several months the squadron carried on maneuvers and training exercises in New Bern, North

Carolina, and Monroe, Louisiana, as well as Quantico. There were rumors the squadron would be assigned to an aircraft carrier, but nothing definite. Finally, immediately after the attack on Pearl Harbor, word came that they would be moving out quickly to the West Coast. On December 11, 1941, there is the first real undercurrent of urgency in Sailer's letters:

> Dear Mother,
>
> We are leaving to-morrow for the West Coast & have been working frantically to get ready. I am sending a trunk home & had to send it C.O.D. because there was such a crowd at the express office that I couldn't wait to fill out the form.
>
> My car was the other big worry as I will have to leave it here. There is a girl [named Floy Larsen] in Washington whom I met & she has arranged to have it stored in the garage of a Mr. Webster who will be away from Washington for a month. . . .
>
> If Betty [his sister] or anyone could use it in Phila & could arrange to get it, there is nothing that would suit me better, as we will probably be gone for quite a while. There is a lot of things stowed in the back of the car, among which is my steel file. I will leave the key to the drawer in the top of the file in the front of it, since the car insurance is in there. Am trying to call you to-night.
>
> Lots of love
> Joe[3]

The next day the squadron headed their airplanes west towards their new base of operations. They flew in a formation of about twenty-four SB2U-3 Vindicator scout bombers, led by Sailer, in a series of hops from Quantico to Montgomery, Alabama, to Jackson, Mississippi, to Dallas, then El Paso, Texas, to Tucson, Arizona, and finally on to the naval base on North Island, San Diego, California. The trip took about nineteen hours of flying time, over a period of a full week, with a few days lost to bad weather.

Life at San Diego was hectic and strenuous at first as the group sought to recover from the hurried trip west as they adjusted to the reality of being in a state of preparation for combat. Within a few days, though, Sailer had settled in and wrote his mother to send him his file of information on stock dividends and his bank statements so he could start work on his 1941 income tax return. He also reminded her about an item that was important enough to him to mention at least three times: the fine new swim fins, which had been mistakenly delivered to him at Quantico, rather than being sent up to Maine as he had expected. He asked her to retrieve them from his car and take them to Maine next summer "because they are lots of fun."[4] He started to gain weight, despite constant training and flying that kept him on the base for six weeks with no break until mid-February. He maintained his keen interest in the family; even in the midst of the crunch to prepare the squadron for the inevitable overseas duty, he took time to correspond with his growing group of nieces and nephews. He wrote several letters to his nephew Bill White, now seven, at one point giving Bill advice on the youngster's ambitious plan to start a vegetable garden:

[M]y advice is to make it just as big as possible, because, unlike you, I am not a bird eater & require lots of food. Also if you are going to feed the whole family and are also including your uncles, it will be a big proposition. In England, when the war started, everyone began to grow a garden & when things got a little scarce, those old vegetables coming out of the ground sure tasted good, in fact much better than any you can buy in the stores.[5]

He remarked to his mother that he "couldn't get over how cute the letter was that [his sister Alice's seven-year-old daughter] Mary Litchfield wrote."[6]

Then, after some time of rumors about reorganizations, Sailer announced that a new squadron, designated VMSB-132, had been formed out of the old one, and he was to be the commanding officer, as of the beginning of March 1942.[7] The new squadron started off with such a crush of paperwork that "everyone was starting to look pale and worn out from being indoors so much." To counter this situation, once the paperwork was caught up, Sailer had the squadron go on marches of five or six miles every day, with a few games of volleyball thrown in for good measure. The remedy worked, and soon Sailer "never felt better & everyone else looks about three times as healthy." He still maintained his low-key approach, even as squadron commander; he evidently did not adopt a more forceful personality than before, except when necessary to get the job done. This system always worked for him, and he won the men over as they came to know and respect him. Edward Wallof, who joined the squadron in San Diego as an enlisted pilot, said:

When I got there, and I met Joe, he seemed kind of meek, and I thought,"he's not much of a guy to be leading a squadron," but there were some rugged individuals in the other squadrons, and Joe turned out to be the best of them all.[8]

He seemed to be feeling relatively settled, rather than worrying about the uncertainty of going off to war; he wrote his mother that he was thinking of the possibility of buying a house in San Diego, partly as an investment opportunity.[9] After a few weeks, he felt the squadron was becoming quite efficient, and the organized engineer in him enjoyed his new leadership duties in a somewhat detached way:

> It is the first time I have ever had a large number of men under me & it is quite interesting to study their reactions. I have quite a complicated card system to keep track of them[,] each man appearing on four different cards.[10]

It was shortly after Sailer assumed command of VMSB-132 that the squadron began training with the type of airplane that it would fly in combat in the South Pacific. Since June of 1941, the predecessor squadron had been doing virtually all of its flying in Chance-Vought SB2U-3 Vindicators, fabric-covered dive-bombers that were rapidly becoming obsolete, and that later were considered below-par "relics" in the fighting at Midway.[11] Beginning in June 1940, though, the Marine Corps began to use a new, superior dive-bomber manufactured by the Douglas Aircraft Company in El Segundo, California. This airplane, officially designated the SBD, for Scout Bomber Douglas, had a metal fuselage, improved performance when carrying a thousand-pound bomb, and a well-designed system for providing speed control and stability during the dive: large flaps under the wings, perforated with large holes to eliminate tail buffeting and to permit the pilot to approach the target in a steep dive, rather than in the shallower glides required in earlier dive-bombers, which exposed the pilots to enemy fire for longer periods.[12] The Douglas company chose an alliterative, and highly appropriate name for its new dive-bomber: the Dauntless. Although it was considered relatively slow and underarmed, it was stable, rugged, responsive to control movements, and its dive brakes permitted it to deliver its destructive payload accurately. Its common nickname summed up the balance of its faults and virtues: "Slow But Deadly."[13]

Once the squadron had SBDs to train with, one activity that Sailer enjoyed greatly and that impressed the squadron members was experimenting with the airplane's Sperry autopilot. Sailer had mastered the device so thoroughly that he could take off and land the plane with the autopilot. Shortly before the squadron left for Guadalcanal, John McEniry flew on Sailer's wing on one occasion at North Island when Sailer landed his SBD with the Sperry device. Sailer also conducted the training on use of the autopilot in the SBD.[14]

In April, Fred Vose came out and spent some time with Sailer, who showed the squadron the 16mm color and sound movie that Sperry had made of Sailer's and Vose's adventures overseas, "Experiences in England." The forty-five-minute film, fairly advanced for its day in the use of color, incorporated a lot of footage that had been shot by the two Sperry men during their tour of duty in England. Narrated by Vose, the movie provided an interesting mix of the aspects of the trip that had caught their fancy—not only scenes of the men and planes associated with testing the bomb sight, but also clear footage of the devastation from German bombing of England, shots of the captured Messerschmit, and footage of a London cabdriver turning his cab in a tight radius, for which Sailer, as ever fascinated by engineering marvels, bribed him with a shilling.[15] The film was used mainly as an information vehicle in-house for Sperry; its mixture of footage was considered somewhat too diverse to be suitable for clients.[16]

Sailer wrote his mother that Vose was eager to show the film to her back in Philadelphia.[17] Vose was not to get the chance to do so, however. On May 1, 1942, he boarded a United Air Lines Mainliner with thirteen other passengers, bound from San Francisco to New York. About five hours out, nearing its scheduled stop at Salt Lake City during a rainstorm, the airplane struck a peak of the Wasatch Mountains; all aboard were killed.[18] Vose, who was forty when he died, left behind a son, Frederic H.E., sixteen, and a daughter, Jane, seven. When Sailer wrote his widow, Henrietta, and sent her a spray of yellow roses, Mrs. Vose wrote back a gracious letter of thanks, saying that Fred had said of Sailer, "[I] certainly wish he was with Sperry. I doubt if I'll ever know a fellow whom I will like so much."[19]

At the end of August Sailer wrote his mother that he had been made a major, which was a relief because some of his contemporaries had been promoted a few months earlier. The good news caused him some concern, though, because "now I am afraid that they may take me out of the squadron & give me some sort of a staff job which I would hate."[20] By this time, the squadron had begun to expand rapidly beyond its initial small size, and, ironically, Sailer finally found some respite from the daily grind of work: He now had a "new executive officer, Major Robertshaw, who comes from outside Philadelphia & who is about the most efficient person I have ever seen. He has been working himself to death ever since being in the squadron & I have had a little spare time." There would be very little opportunity to enjoy the spare time, though; it was clear to Sailer at this point that the squadron was slated to move out soon.[21]

Throughout this period the training was intense. Beginning in early August, the squadron had switched from the first model of Dauntless, the SBD-1, to the improved SBD-3, which had greater fuel capacity for longer range, and had upgraded guns for the pilot and gunner. This was the model that they would fly in combat, and "the one aircraft model which would truly become the work-horse of the Pacific War in the year following the Japanese attack on Pearl Harbor."[22] The pilots and gunners put the new models through their paces in section tactics, cross-country flying, engineering, night flights, flights with oxygen, ground strafing, and, foremost in tactical importance, dive-bombing, using miniature five-pound smoke bombs over circular targets on the ground near Camp Miramar.[23]

Sailer managed to send just one more letter to his mother, on September 28, 1942. At this point it was only a question of when the squadron would be sent into combat. This last letter, while reflecting such mundane matters as Sailer's concern about keeping his financial affairs in order, has an air of finality:

Dear Mother,
    I have made out a Power of Attorney and a Last Will and Testament which I am enclosing. I

will also send my note book containing the list of stocks, insurance etc. to you so that you can take care of various premiums etc. all of which I am afraid will be quite a job. I have collected so much money lately, having no expenses to speak of, that I decided it would be a good thing to buy some bonds & have purchased one for each of my nieces & nephews with the exception of John & Marion's baby since I did not know his name. Will you please buy one for him out of the $2,000 check enclosed which is also money for insurance etc. (income tax). By the way my bank balance is still off $100 because you never deposited that check I sent to you last Christmas. I won another bond on a raffle which I am sending to you now.

We are all ready to leave now & will probably be on our way shortly.

With lots of love,
Joe[24]

CHAPTER FIVE
GUADALCANAL

Before beginning the story of Joe Sailer's brief but extra-ordinary time at Guadalcanal, it is necessary to provide some framework for the events that took place there in November and December of 1942. With the surprise attack at Pearl Harbor on December 7, 1941, the Japanese seized the initiative and held it for some time, expanding their domain steadily into the Pacific Ocean to the east. By May of 1942, Japanese forces had made an unbroken string of conquests, including Hong Kong, Wake Island, Singapore, Burma, and the Philippines. But in June, in a stunning naval and air battle, the Japanese ran into disaster as they attempted to provoke the American Navy's aircraft carriers into a decisive and destructive battle to defend the United States base at Midway Island, a remote outpost about a thousand miles from Pearl Harbor. Through a combination of brilliant tactics, dogged determination, and great luck, the Americans held off the enemy fleet, sinking four of the Japanese aircraft carriers while losing only one.

The Japanese had planned to establish their air operations at Midway; the defeat there left them looking for an alternative location. The site they chose was the largest of the Solomons, a widely scattered group of 922 islands in the South Pacific about a thousand miles northeast of Australia. First settled thousands of years ago, the islands were encountered by explorers from Spanish-occupied Peru in 1568, who bestowed upon them Spanish names, such as Santa Isabel, Santa Ana, and Santa Catalina. Reflecting the Moorish influence in Spain, the Spaniards named the largest island Wadi-al-Canar, after the home village in southern Spain of the island's discoverer. After years of European exploration in the late eighteenth and nineteenth centuries, Great Britain in 1899 established the British Solomon Islands Protectorate and assumed control over the entire island group. The name of the largest island earlier had been Anglicized to Guadalcanar, and by the end of the nineteenth century it had assumed its present form of Guadalcanal.

The largest of the Solomon Islands are arranged in what could be considered as two roughly parallel but gently curving rows oriented along a northwest-southeast line. The slightly bulging framework of the group surrounds a long expanse of ocean called New Georgia Sound, more popularly known by its wartime appellation, "the Slot." Guadalcanal sits at the bottom of this pattern, almost at the southeast extreme of the group. The island is shaped like an irregular potato or cucumber, about thirty miles wide by ninety miles long. The interior is mountainous, with some peaks rising over a mile. The landscape also includes dense jungles, inactive volcanic cones, and short rivers that flood easily in heavy rains. The northern coast, with a climate milder than the southern, receives about 180 days of rain per year. Humidity is high, and the temperature ranges between seventy and eighty-eight degrees Fahrenheit during the year.[1]

Beginning in late June of 1942, Japanese planners stationed on the occupied islands of Gavutu and Tulagi in the Solomons began scouting for a suitable location for an airfield. Observed by the vigilant and well-concealed Coastwatchers, native scouts organized and trained by the Australians to provide information about Japanese movements,[2] these advance men settled in a flat grove near the northern coast of Guadalcanal.[3] Soon, initial shipments of troops and equipment were ferried ashore from neighboring bases, and construction of the air facility was in progress.

The Americans decided by early July that they would launch an amphibious invasion to uproot the Japanese from this new expansion to the east. The First Marine Division landed at Guadalcanal and smaller islands on August 7. On Guadalcanal, the Marines met little resistance on land, and by August 8 they had taken control of the airfield and begun to put it into shape to serve their own interests. On August 12, the first U.S. plane landed on the runway of what was soon to be named Henderson Field, after Marine Major Lofton R. Henderson, squadron commander of VMSB-241, who was killed in action leading his dive-bomber pilots at Midway on June 4, 1942.[4]

For the next few weeks the Marines fought fiercely on land against the dug-in Japanese defenders, who were determined to regain control of the island and the airfield. The American aviators at Henderson Field, who represented the Marine Corps and, eventually, the army and navy, operated as best they could under the harsh and hazardous conditions that prevailed. Dubbed the "Cactus Air Force" after the military codename CACTUS for Guadalcanal, the pilots searched daily for invaders attempting to re-supply and reinforce the Japanese troops via the "Tokyo Express," as the Americans came to call the convoys of transports and escorting warships that traveled down the Slot from Japanese bases at Rabaul on New Britain, and elsewhere.

Besides bearing materiel and men for the besieged army on Guadalcanal, the Japanese navy ships carried weapons with which they sporadically attempted to neutralize the aerial opposition that was emanating daily from Henderson Field. Coupled with ground-based mortar shellings from Japanese units called "Millimeter Mike" by the American airmen, and with aerial bombings that occurred in some form almost every night, the ocean-based artillery bombardments on occasion were augmented to levels of great destructive power. One such instance stood out for its fury as unparalleled not only in the campaign for Guadalcanal, but as virtually without equal throughout the entire war.

Long after dark, close to midnight on the night of October 13, 1942, the Japanese navy positioned two battleships, *Kongo* and *Haruna*, within range of the air base, and, after their aircraft had dropped high-intensity flares to mark the target, the two ships' sixteen guns began zeroing in on Henderson Field. They soon found the range, and, for more than an hour the huge guns propelled a total of more than 900 fourteen-inch shells, some high-explosive and some armor-piercing, into the area of the airfield. The unimaginable terror this great bombardment caused to the men in their foxholes was matched by the actual destruction. Samuel Griffith in *The Battle for Guadalcanal* stated simply: "Few bombardments of World War II equaled this in the amount of large calibre ammunition fired in a few minutes more than an hour on so small a target."[5]

The tangible devastation caused by this unprecedented attack was all too easily measured: of 39 operational SBDs,

34 were destroyed or knocked out of commission; 16 of 40 Wildcat fighters were destroyed, and the 24 others were damaged. In human terms, there were 60 casualties, of whom 41 were killed.[6] Most pertinent to the story of Joseph Sailer was the terrible loss sustained by one squadron of dive-bombers. VMSB-141, which had arrived bit by bit on Guadalcanal from late September up to the very day of the shelling, lost five officers, including its squadron commander, executive officer, and flight officer, in this one deadly night on the ground. This squadron, barely arrived on the scene, was eviscerated before it had much of a chance to become oriented and effective. Eventually, of forty-one pilots that arrived for combat, the squadron lost eighteen killed or missing in action, and another nine to injuries or illness.[7] Thus, by late October, there was a desperate need for more airplanes, and for pilots to fly them into combat.

On October 13, 1942, the same day as the terrible shelling of Henderson Field that devastated VMSB-141, Joe Sailer and his squadron, VMSB-132, embarked at San Diego aboard a troopship code-named the USS *Mumu*, actually the luxury vessel *Lurline* of the Matson line, bound for the South Pacific with about 6,000 troops on board. The twin-stack, 630-foot vessel was in fine condition and quite new, having been launched into cruising service just ten years before. Although the ship was far more crowded than a commercial cruise, the conditions on board were fine in many ways; the officers' meals were served by the stewards of the line, and the food was of the same excellent quality enjoyed by passengers in peacetime, until fresh milk and other items ran out about two-thirds of the way across.[8]

The squadron at this point had twenty-seven Marine officers and 245 Marine enlisted men, with a few Navy personnel attached.[9] The enlisted men of VMSB-132 slept twelve to a stateroom in four sets of triple bunks. In the grand ballroom, plywood covered the mirrored walls, but the elegant chandeliers still glittered from the ceiling as reminders of the ship's peacetime grandeur. During the twelve-day voyage to the South Pacific, the officers played a lot of bridge and conducted combat training sessions for the pilots and other men. In the classes on identification of Japanese ships and planes, the silhouettes would be flashed on a screen for a split second to see how fast the men could identify them and count them accurately. They kept in shape with physical exercise up on the deck.

During one of the training sessions on board the ship, Sailer showed his rarely evident temper. He laid out a series of steps for a particular procedure, then called on Lieutenant Simpson to repeat the steps of the procedure. Simpson got one step out of order, and Sailer snapped at him sharply. The squadron commander seemed quiet and mild-mannered, but had a firm sense of command when the occasion arose.[10]

Because of the ship's great speed of about twenty knots, it did not have to travel in a convoy but merely zigzagged to avoid submarines,[11] and the trip was uneventful, except for an epidemic of seasickness.[12] The *Lurline* arrived on October 28 at its destination of Noumea, on the island of New Caledonia, where the United States had a large headquarters and supply base.

On October 29, while much of the squadron stayed behind under Major Robertshaw, living in tents on a hill overlooking the city, Sailer, along with three of his pilots and their gunners, left Noumea in the first wave of flights ferrying replacements to Guadalcanal.[13] They were driven over fifty miles to the airfield at Tontouta, from which they were flown about 400 miles to the island of Espiritu Santo in the New Hebrides. After an overnight stay there, they were ferried during the night in a DC-3 (R4D) to Henderson Field, with no escort or fighter protection; their only cover was the darkness. After the four and one-half-hour flight, the plane dropped its passengers off in the darkness at Guadalcanal, and was gone within thirty minutes. When Joe Sailer and the first contingent from his squadron finally set foot on the island, it was November 1.

At this time the military action on the island was in a relatively calm phase. On October 26, the Japanese had failed in their second attempt to capture Henderson Field. The desperate struggle for control of Guadalcanal had been going on for about three months, fought on both sides by troops in the jungle, by sailors in the waters of the Slot, and by the pilots and crews of the bombers and fighters based on land and on carriers. Both sides had scored transitory victories and suffered stinging defeats. There was no single battle for control of Guadalcanal, but rather a string of conflicts that together amounted to the campaign to win dominion over the island and its airfield.

In the bloody fighting on land, the American Marines of the First Division had driven the Japanese army units into defensive positions back in the jungle. At sea, the results were mixed. In early August, just after the American landing, a surprise attack sank four American ships and damaged three others in the disastrous Battle of Savo Island. Later in that month, in the course of continuing attempts to bolster their army troops and neutralize Henderson Field, the Japanese sent a large fleet of reinforcements toward the island. This time, in the Battle of the

Eastern Solomons, the Americans had the upper hand, sinking a Japanese carrier and two other ships, while sustaining damage to the carrier *Enterprise*.

In October, in the Battle of Cape Esperance, the two navies clashed at night when the U.S. Navy surprised a Japanese cruiser force, resulting in the loss of four Japanese ships and three American vessels. Then, in the larger Battle of Santa Cruz, on October 26, Vice Admiral William F. Halsey Jr., sent his two carrier forces, centered on the carriers *Enterprise* and *Hornet*, to intercept the Japanese force that was to support the next attempt to take Henderson Field back from the Americans. In this major confrontation, the *Enterprise* was damaged and the *Hornet* ultimately was sunk; the Japanese had two carriers and one cruiser knocked out of action for a period of several weeks, and lost nearly 100 planes and 148 airmen.[14] However, despite the Americans' severe losses, they once again had repelled a Japanese drive to retake the island and its critically important airfield. Now the stage was set for the climactic naval battle that would determine the ultimate course of the campaign.

During the few days before the crucial battle was joined, as more of the squadron's pilots flew SBDs over to Henderson Field, or were flown there in transport planes, Sailer and his early arrivals flew frequent search and observation missions. On November 2, Sailer took an SBD-3 up for an observation flight to familiarize himself with the area and to conduct a general sector search for enemy shipping, aircraft activity, and other matters of interest. In the rear seat was Technical Sergeant Howard Stanley, the radio-gunner who had been flying with him regularly since May of 1942 in San Diego, where they had flown in

SBD-1s and SBD-3s together in the early days of the new squadron's training. Stanley, a twenty-year-old from Ahoskie, North Carolina, seventy miles south of Norfolk, Virginia, had finished high school, and had a scholarship to go to art school, but was more interested in airplanes than art. He already had a private pilot's license when he enlisted in the Marine Corps at seventeen. Now, after extensive training in the States, he was the squadron's chief radioman, and was to be in the rear seat for twenty-four out of the twenty-six flights Sailer would make over the next five weeks, including every attack flight except the final one on December 7. On their first flight at Guadalcanal, the major gave Stanley "a grin from the front cockpit that gave me more courage and confidence than anything else in the world could have given."[15]

That first sector search turned up no sign of the enemy, and Sailer and Stanley returned to Henderson Field after a flight of more than four hours. There was not much respite on the ground, where conditions were never good. There was a scant supply of food, variously reported as consisting of canned lamb's tongue, onion sandwiches, sausage, corned beef, Spam, dried potatoes, and dried eggs, and lots of rice left behind by the Japanese who abandoned the airfield when the Marines landed in August. At one point, the squadron could not even get a lister bag of water, so pilots had to take off before dawn without a cup of coffee, or even so much as a drink of water, until Major Robertshaw managed to secure the needed item.[16] It usually was not possible to have hot meals for breakfast, because firing up the stoves in the early morning darkness would expose the cooks to Japanese snipers.[17] Many men, including Sailer, were plagued by diarrhea, and they suffered from malaria despite the preventive quinine pills; the Solomon Islands were and still are one of the worst areas in the world for malaria, borne by the hordes of ever-present mosquitoes. Everyone lived in tents, with foxholes nearby to duck into during the all too frequent aerial harassment attacks. By the time VMSB-132 arrived, the Marines had learned their lesson about foxhole assignments, and ensured that the squadron's most senior officers did not share a tent or foxhole, after the leadership of VMSB-141 was wiped out in one catastrophic night of shelling on October 13–14.

On most days there were attacks by formations of high-flying enemy bombers. At night the Japanese often sent over a bomber dubbed "Washing Machine Charlie" because of the rough, unsynchronized drone of its propellers.[18] There was heavy artillery, called "Pistol Pete," well back behind the Japanese lines, directing its explosive shells at Henderson Field. Although the Cactus Air Force and the other American forces did their best to suppress these various forms of deadly harassment, there inevitably was a toll taken in lack of sleep and general anxiety.[19] Sailer, like all of the pilots, became tired from lack of sleep, and, during the heaviest periods, from the sheer exhaustion that resulted from dawn-to-dusk flights. He had never been a very large man; at twenty-four, when he was issued his civilian transport pilot's license, he had been listed at five feet eleven inches and 155 pounds. Now, his weight dropped substantially, to the point that he had to tighten his trousers up with a long tail of belt showing, and the pants in large folds like pleats.[20] There is no indication that he was pushed close to a breaking point, though; he always remained cool, level-headed, and focused clearly

Joe Sailer's father, Dr. Joseph Sailer, in 1913.

Joseph Sailer Jr., at the summer home of his grandfather, George Strawbridge, in Camden, Maine, about 1912.

Joe Sailer's mother, Mary Lowber Sailer.

Spring Bank, the Philadelphia summer home of Joseph Sailer Jr.'s grandfather, John Welsh, shown here in the 19th century.

The Wilderness, Philadelphia home where Joe Sailer's mother, Mary Lowber Strawbridge, was born in 1875.

The Forecastle, summer home of the Sailer family in Camden, Maine. This picture was probably taken in the early 1920s.

The Sailer children, about 1919. Left to right: Anne West, Albin Penington, Elizabeth Twells, Priscilla Sparks, John, Joseph Jr., Mary, Alice.

Joseph Sailer Jr.'s aunt Anne West Strawbridge with her autogiro, probably taken near Philadelphia between 1936 and 1941.

Joseph Sailer Jr. at the helm of a sailboat at Camden, Maine, in the 1930s.

Joseph Sailer Jr. on the float at his mother's cabin on Lake Megunticook, Camden, Maine, with his nephew Bill White, about 1938.

Ledlie Newlin, in or around Philadelphia, 1937.

Joe Sailer's Ford roadster, San Diego, 1931. His note on the back of the picture says: "My ford, the finest in America."

Joseph Sailer, Jr. (right) and his Marine buddy from San Diego training, Martin A. Severson, taken in April 1937, probably in or near Philadelphia.

Joseph Sailer Jr. (fifth from left) with his training squadron in front of a Vought O2U Corsair at San Diego, probably 1931.

A Curtiss OC-2 used by the Marine Corps in training
at the San Diego Naval Air Station, 1931.
(National Archives No. 80-G- 650679)

Joseph Sailer Jr. (left) ready to fly in training at San Diego.

Joseph Sailer Jr. entering the
cockpit during training in
New York.

H.M.S. *Lincoln,* the former United States destroyer converted and given to the British, on which
Joseph Sailer Jr. traveled to England in October 1940.
(The Trustees of the Imperial War Museum, London, No. FL-3266)

Smoke marks the explosion of a bomb dropped from 8,000 feet onto an armed German
supply ship at Tyboron Harbor, Denmark, April 30, 1941, in the RAF's first combat use of
the Sperry O-1 bomb sight.
(London News Chronicle, June 6, 1941, courtesy of Franklin Joseph)

S.S. *Lurline*, the former luxury liner converted to a troop ship, which took Joseph Sailer Jr. and his squadron to the South Pacific in 1942.
(Steamship Historical Society Collection, University of Baltimore Library, No. 706A)

Major L.B. Robertshaw, executive officer (later commanding officer) of VMSB-132, shown here at Espiritu Santo in October 1943.
(National Archives 80-G-54759)

Howard Stanley, Joseph Sailer Jr.'s regular radio-gunner at Guadalcanal, shown here in 1943.
(Courtesy of Howard Stanley)

A Marine Corps SBD and her crew on Guadalcanal in June 1943.
(National Archives 80-G-54910)

In the background, beached Japanese transports burn at Guadalcanal after the battle of mid-November 1942.
(National Archives 80-G-30517)

An SBD returning to Henderson Field on Guadalcanal in June 1943, showing the perforated landing flaps extended. The dive flaps, which are similar in appearance, are located directly above the landing flaps on the trailing edge of the wing surface.
(National Archives 80-G-54900)

A Marine SBD squadron warms up at Henderson Field on December 10, 1942, before a strike.

(*National Archives 127-GR-89-108572*)

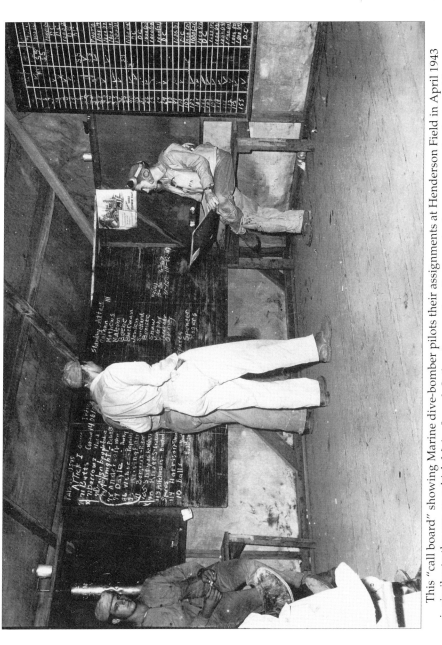

This "call board" showing Marine dive-bomber pilots their assignments at Henderson Field in April 1943 is similar to the one on which Major Joseph Sailer, Jr. occasionally erased other names and substituted his own.

(National Archives 127-GW-55783)

Oblique view of Henderson Field on Guadalcanal, taken shortly after the U.S. invasion in August 1942. Savo Island is in the background.
(National Archives 80-G-224153)

Joseph Sailer Jr. (right) with Fred Vose in a scene from the 1942 Sperry film "Experiences in England" as they prepare to fly to Canada with Sperry bomb sights in 1940, en route to England. Crates of the equipment are visible in the background.

One of the beached Japanese transports that was bombed by Joseph Sailer Jr.'s dive-bomber squadron and others during the battle of mid-November 1942 at Guadalcanal.
(Official U.S. Marine Corps photograph 012-2454-94)

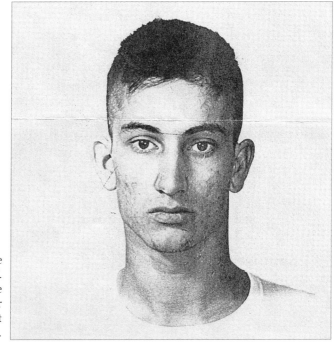

Photograph from the military file of James W. Alexander, the substitute gunner on Joseph Sailer Jr.'s final flight at Guadalcanal.

Visit of Joseph Sailer Jr.'s family to the Sperry Gyroscope Company's new plant at Great Neck, Long Island, February 17, 1945. Left to right: Bill Harcum of Sperry; Sailer's sister, Elizabeth (Betty) Churchman; his brother-in-law, Lawrence Litchfield; his sister, Alice Litchfield; his brother John; his mother; Robert B. Lea, Sperry's vice president for sales (and son-in-law of Elmer Sperry, founder of the company).

Joseph Sailer Jr. with his pipe in a scene taken in England from the 1942 Sperry film.

This color comic strip appeared in the *New York Herald Tribune* on December 31, 1944.

on the mission at hand. He did allow himself one special dispensation to battle the drudgery and fatigue: Just about every morning he stopped by the sick bay and saw Lieutenant Victor Falk, a Navy doctor who was flight surgeon for VMSB-141, the squadron that had been devastated by the shelling on the night of October 13–14. Dr. Falk supplied Sailer with a dose of elixir terpin hydrate, a cough medicine that had the bitter orange taste, and at least some of the alcohol content, of cointreau.[21]

Sailer did his best to look out for the other pilots and enlisted men in the squadron. Together with his resourceful and dedicated supply officer, Lieutenant Ernie Brenner, he managed to secure scarce but crucial items that would not have seemed of much consequence back in the United States, such as rags to wipe the windshields of the airplanes. To deal with the shortage of satisfying food, Sailer had Brenner take advantage of an unusual characteristic of the squadron: very few of its members were drinkers, so the supply officer had the squadron's ration of rum to work with for barter, and he managed to trade it for ice cream, a much-appreciated luxury that provided a welcome contrast to Spam and nondescript dried foods.[22]

The squadron commander was by no means a pushover, though; on one occasion he heard some of his men talking about when they might be going home. Sailer told them to knock it off; "You're here to fight and until we're ready to go, you don't talk about going home."[23]

Despite the hardships and the general lack of amenities, the dive-bomber pilots, like their colleagues in torpedo bombers and fighters, managed to function in top form when the chips were down. Though each mission was, of course, unique in some way, and each pilot and gunner had their own ways of doing things, the typical mission of VMSB-132 followed a general pattern. The "typical" mission outlined here is an attack against shipping; there were, of course, other types of flights, such as search missions and attacks on ground positions. This description incorporates information about the specific procedures used by Sailer and Stanley.

Once the targets had been named, either from reports generated by search flights or by intelligence reports from the Coastwatchers, the pilots would go to the Henderson Field operations hut for a briefing. The pilot and gunner would then walk over to the runway and meet at the airplane assigned to them for that flight; there was no telling which SBD they would get. The parachutes, which were left in the plane from flight to flight, might be soaking wet when the men got in; they wouldn't know if the chutes would work if needed.

As the leader, Sailer took off first, out over the water, then circled around waiting for the other planes in the group to form up on him. Once they had gained a little altitude, the pilot and gunner snapped on their parachutes. They normally left the front and rear canopies open throughout the whole flight, because the temperatures were warm enough, and the open canopies allowed a quick exit in the event of an emergency. Not long into the flight, Sailer test-fired his two .50-caliber guns that were fixed in place and synchronized through the propeller, and Stanley test-fired the two movable .30-calibers on his turret in the back. Once the formation had been established and the group was heading out to its destination, Sailer often would let Stanley take over flying, using the duplicate set of controls from the rear seat—Stanley had his pilot's license when he enlisted, and above all had wanted the Marines to send him to flight school. Sailer was planning to arrange for this after their tour at Guadalcanal.[24]

On many missions, the target was enemy ships that had been sighted somewhere out in the Slot. The SBDs could seek them out anywhere within their effective range of 300 miles from Henderson Field. Once the American planes made visual contact with the enemy, Sailer gave Stanley a coded message, which Stanley sent by telegraph key back to the operations center on Guadalcanal. Besides alerting headquarters as to the status of the current attack, this message gave the people on Guadalcanal some idea of what to expect that night in the way of shelling from Japanese ships that were heading into range for that purpose.

The formation of SBDs (together with TBFs, fighters, and others, depending on the occasion) would normally fly the early portion of the mission at 8,000 to 10,000 feet, where supplemental oxygen was not required. Then, as they approached the target area, they would climb to their initial attack altitude of 12,000 feet or somewhat higher. If they went much above 12,000, they used oxygen masks to avoid the headaches and lightheadedness that came from the thin atmosphere at that altitude.

From the attack altitude, the dive-bombers would start descending at 1,000 to 2,000 feet per minute, picking up speed in the steep downward slope. At least in Sailer's squadron, the SBDs did not dive in a single steep line down to the target. Rather, they descended in a series of steps, called "stairstepping" by some pilots, so they got progressively steeper in their dives. In this way, the pilots avoided the danger of overshooting the targets in a single, miscalculated dive slope. Also, if they got too steep too soon, the plane might begin to skid and become hard to control. They didn't get into their final, steepest dive until they were down to just under 7,000 feet.

Throughout the diving maneuvers, the ships' anti-aircraft guns would be firing, but the Japanese at this time did not have altitude radar to measure the airplanes' vertical range. As soon as the flak began to get close to the planes' actual altitude, the pilots dropped down to a lower level, in their stairstepping maneuver, which, in addition to providing greater precision in the diving approach, helped them avoid the shell bursts. After the stairstepping moves had been repeated once or twice, the pilots would be in their final dive on the ships.[25]

The Dauntless pilots would have coordinated among themselves how to divide up the targets. One three-plane section might select one column of ships, another section a different column, depending on the configuration in which the ships were arranged. Sailer, as leader, would dive first, followed closely by the remainder of his section. Sailer would reduce power and open his dive brakes. These were the perforated metal sections of the upper and lower surfaces of the wings' trailing edges. When opened, the outboard sections of both wing surfaces opened to form a "V" with the wing's trailing edge, assisted by a center section under the fuselage that opened downward, so that a total of five wing sections were acting to produce drag to slow the descent of the diving SBD. The dive had to be controlled and stable in order to drop the bomb on target. Without the dive brakes, the Dauntless would plummet down at over 400 knots, and could not be controlled with the needed precision. With the brakes deployed, the speed would drop to about 200 knots, so the airplane could be kept in steady trim for the bombing run.

As he guided the plane down toward the targeted ship, Sailer had to ignore whatever flak was bursting around him; at this point, it was critical to keep the plane steady on course. He had a primitive sort of bomb sight that was built through the windshield, a device like a telescope with triple magnification and cross-hairs, nothing like the elaborate gyro-controlled bomb sights made by Sperry and Norden. He had to raise his seat with a lever, lean forward, and keep one hand and one eye glued to the bomb sight. He used that view to maintain the plane straight on course for the ship below, so he couldn't see the altimeter.[26] When the time was right, he told Stanley to start counting down the altitude in thousands of feet, "ten-nine-eight-seven" and so on as they made their descent.[27] As they approached the enemy ship, the pilot would fire his twin .50-caliber machine guns, with the intent of making the ship's gunners dive for cover, thereby suppressing the anti-aircraft fire.[28]

When his plane had dived down to about the 2,000-foot level, Sailer would reach out with his left hand to a small knob with a lever on it. He would pull back sharply on this lever, which would release the bomb.[29] They couldn't go much lower for the drop, or they would be in danger of being hit by shrapnel from the explosion. If they dropped from much higher, the chances of a hit on the target were greatly reduced. The range for various pilots varied from about 1,500 feet to as high as 3,000 or 4,000. In any event, once the bomb was away, the Dauntless would jump up and ahead from the sudden loss of the 1,000-pound weight. Sailer would close the dive flaps, apply full throttle, and pull up sharply out of the dive. At this point, the positive g-force would cause the blood to drain down from their heads, and Sailer and Stanley would both black out for a few seconds.[30]

When the plane came back under normal g-force in the climb, the blood flowed back to their heads and they regained consciousness. The plane would still be pulling back up. They wouldn't return to high altitude at this point, in order to keep the enemy fighter planes from attacking from below. There was a different danger from staying low, though: The Japanese ships could fire their large-diameter guns, and the shells would throw up a wall of water that could knock down a low-flying airplane. Still, the preference was to stay low until the airplanes were out of range of enemy fighters and then to climb to 3,000 or 4,000 feet for the flight back to Henderson Field.

As long as they were in range of the Japanese fighters, the Dauntless crews had to maintain sharp vigilance and attend to their front and rear guns. Sailer's gunner, Stanley, had many occasions to shoot at Zeroes, and once was able to claim a kill. As Stanley recounted the incident, a Zero had approached Sailer's Dauntless from below and fired at the airplane's rear. The Zero came up close behind the Dauntless, then rolled onto its back to peel away. At this point, according to Stanley, "when he turned over on the back, the whole bottom was exposed and I was leading on him and I had a good shot on him, and I just held on to him and killed him, and you could see the smoke and he went down and went in."[31]

Keeping the guns ready to fire was not a matter of routine. The tropical humidity caused corrosion of the metal parts of the ammunition belts. Often, after a couple of shots were fired the belt would jam. After one flight with this experience and no remedy at hand, Stanley instituted a procedure to deal with the problem—he had all the gunners wear screwdrivers on strings around their necks. When the guns jammed, they could eject the jammed shell with the screwdriver and get the gun firing again right away.

By the time they made it back to Henderson Field after making contact with the enemy, the Dauntless usually had an abundance of bullet holes in it. The sturdy, reliable "Slow But Deadly" usually was not fazed by these penetrations, and the ground crews back at Henderson would patch them up with aluminum strips topped off with a green primer paint. The result was that some of the planes looked like "checkerboards," with green strips dotting the blue fuselage after a few flights.

When the flights returned, sometimes in daylight and sometimes after dark, the returning pilots and gunners would line up for chow. One thing that endeared Sailer to his men was that he never cut to the front of these lines or asserted any privileges of rank to get his food faster; he stood in line with the men, and ate what they ate, wherever he could find a seat.[32]

Of course, there were many variations to this "typical" scenario for a mission. On attacks against shipping, the Dauntless carried a single 1,000-pound bomb underneath the fuselage, to do maximum damage to a single, relatively small target. During the occasional missions to bomb enemy ground positions on Guadalcanal or neighboring islands, the plane would carry one 500-pound bomb in the center, and two 100-pound bombs, one on each wing. In this case, the object was to do the maximum damage to an enemy encampment or other ground facility, and with three bombs the plane could inflict more damage and create more shrapnel over a wider area than with a single 1,000-pound missile.

Another variation from the normal routine was to fly at night. Normally, the SBDs attacked during daylight hours, if fighter cover was available. During daylight, it was much easier to locate and aim at the targets. However, in some situations, such as attacks on New Georgia or on shipping far out in the Slot, the SBDs could fly beyond the range of their fighter coverage. In those cases, the SBDs might launch an attack at night to avoid running into Zeroes when no fighters were escorting the American planes. On some other occasions, a flight was launched during daylight and did not make it back in until after dark. This was the case, with tragic consequences for one pilot, on December 1. Most often, though, the flights went out and returned in daylight.

Sailer went on another search mission on November 3, which proved largely uneventful; he reported one plane down on the beach just north of Tunibuli. On November 5, Sailer and Lieutenant Walter A. Eck went on a successful mission to drop a message to friendly forces on the ground. During this flight they reported one enemy destroyer 210 miles from Henderson Field.

Then, on November 6, Lieutenant Eck, while on a sector search near New Georgia, reported an enemy task force of sixteen destroyers spread out over a range of 200 to 215 miles from Henderson Field, all heading west toward Guadalcanal. This was another run of the Tokyo Express, bringing reinforcing troops and supplies to the aid of the beleaguered Japanese ground forces on Guadalcanal. By the next day, the ships were 100 miles out, and it was time for the Cactus Air Force to attack. Most of the other pilots of VMSB-132 had not yet arrived at Henderson Field, so for his first attack flight Sailer led a group of SBDs piloted by men of other squadrons. He coordinated his attack with Navy Lieutenant Harold H. "Swede" Larsen, who led a group of three TBF torpedo planes of VT-8. By this time the enemy task force was made up of nine destroyers and one light cruiser. Lieutenant Amedeo Sandretto of VMSB-141 got a direct hit on the cruiser with his SBD's bomb despite heavy anti-aircraft fire, and Lieutenants Larsen and Evarts of VT-8 got torpedo hits on the cruiser and one destroyer. After Sandretto got his hit he noticed that three Japanese float Zeroes were attacking Sailer; Sandretto turned back and together his plane and Sailer's managed to drive off the attacking planes. The Americans' fighter protection of Army P-39s downed five Japanese float biplanes during this mission. One American pilot, Lieutenant Sullivan of VMSB-141, failed to return.

Besides Sailer's first attack mission, November 7 brought reinforcements for VMSB-132. The squadron's remaining pilots arrived from Espiritu Santo, where they had picked up a group of nine SBDs that had been removed from the carrier *Hornet* before its loss at sea on October 27.[33] The newly arrived pilots, led by Major Robertshaw, were Staff Sergeant Edward J. Wallof and Second Lieutenants Archie D. "Hap" Simpson, John E. Sperzel, Russell L. Janson, John H. McEniry Jr., Charles E. Kollman, George B. "Jug" Herlihy, and Horace C. Baum Jr. Wallof was one of only two enlisted pilots in the squadron. They had the same duties and flying skills as the officers; it was easier administratively to add enlisted pilots than officers, because of limitations on the authorized number of officers.[34] In any event, by all accounts he and his colleague, Master Sergeant Kenneth Gordon, were indistinguishable from the officer-pilots, and in fact they both later received commissions.

On November 8, Sailer and Lieutenant Cruger L. "Curley" Bright (who had arrived on November 6) flew their SBDs out on a four-hour search mission, but spotted only friendly ships—five destroyers and four light cruisers.[35] Then, on November 10, Lieutenant Bright, on a sector search early in the day, reported five Japanese destroyers heading for the island from 210 miles out. Sailer was tapped to lead an attack group against this latest attempt to land more men and supplies. The other pilots in the attack group were Wallof, Janson, Simpson, Baum, Gordon, and men from other Marine scout bombing squadrons. The aircraft located the ships 170 miles out and delivered their bombs, but the visibility was poor and the anti-aircraft fire heavy, and no hits were reported. Wallof, who was flying just about twenty feet to the side of the squadron commander, years later described his impression of Sailer during this first attack by the squadron on enemy ships:

> [W]e were flying over five destroyers and we were just about 10,000 feet, and all of a sudden, the anti-aircraft started coming up and you could see the puffs below, and all of a sudden one came off right between us and you could hear it ring in your ears, but old Joe just turned around with a big grin on his face and kept weaving on.[36]

The main action for the dive-bombers in November was yet to begin.

CHAPTER SIX
NOVEMBER–DECEMBER 1942

As is made clear in many accounts of the naval conflicts in the South Pacific (and elsewhere), it is easy to overestimate the losses of the opposition. At the conclusion of the Battle of the Santa Cruz Islands, the Japanese concluded that the Americans had lost four carriers, one battleship, and 200 or more aircraft,[1] when the actual losses were one carrier (the *Hornet*) sunk, and one (the *Enterprise*) badly damaged, but destined to be repaired so quickly as to rejoin the fray much more rapidly than could reasonably have been expected. The Americans lost a total of eighty-one aircraft.[2] Thus, partly because of this over-optimistic assessment of the situation, and partly because of a realization that time was running out on their plans to regain control of Guadalcanal, the Japanese military planners set in motion one more great run of the Tokyo Express—a major reinforcement operation undertaken in preparation for a final offensive that was to take place in December.[3]

The Japanese plans called for the landing at Cape Esperance and Tassafaronga of eleven troop transport ships carrying about 7,000 soldiers along with supplies for many more troops, including masses of food and ammunition.[4]

The escort of fighting ships included the carrier *Junyo*, accompanied by four *Kongo* class battleships, three heavy cruisers, three light cruisers, and twenty-one destroyers.[5] Two of the battleships, *Kirishima* and *Hiei*, were designated to blast Henderson Field with their sixteen massive guns firing fourteen-inch explosive shells.[6]

On November 12th, lieutenants William Hronek and Walter Eck spotted a Japanese force that they reported as two small aircraft carriers, one with planes on the flight deck, and two destroyers.[7] Sailer led one attack late in the day, with Major Robertshaw, Eck, Hronek, and Bright, and Master Sergeant Gordon. The Dauntlesses had proceeded only about eighty-five miles toward the targets when darkness and "exceptionally bad weather" forced them to return to Henderson Field. There would be no shortage of action for the next few days, however.

Very late on the 12th, and in the early morning hours of the 13th, the ferocious Naval Battle of Guadalcanal got under way at close quarters in darkness and confusion. There were considerable losses on both sides: the Americans lost five destroyers and two cruisers, including, in a catastrophe itself of historic proportions, virtually the entire crew of the cruiser *Juneau*.[8] The Japanese ultimately lost three ships, including, of most interest for the story of Joe Sailer, the first of their battleships to be lost during the war.[9] But the Americans won a major tactical victory in that the U.S. Navy, despite its losses, had correctly gauged the enemy's plan to shell Henderson Field into oblivion. The Navy's leadership devoted great efforts to foiling this design. As a result, the Marine pilots based at Henderson were free to join their comrades from the Navy in launching wave after wave of attacks on the transports and their remaining Japanese escorts.

Thus the SBDs and fighters were able to resume their operations before dawn on the 13th, this time with some major targets within range during daylight. On Sailer's first sortie of the day, he led Kollman and Simpson on a tracking mission to survey the scene in the waters off Guadalcanal. They found damaged American ships tending to survivors and witnessed the sinking of the Japanese destroyer *Yudachi* by the damaged American heavy cruiser *Portland*. But Sailer and his VMSB-132 pilots also reported the biggest news from their perspective—a Japanese battleship of the *Kongo* class, just eight miles from the American ships and thirty miles from Henderson Field, with smoke coming from its forward gun turrets and its rear turrets dangling. It wasn't clear at first if this was a U.S. or a Japanese ship, so Howard Stanley, Sailer's gunner, took his signal gun and flashed the recognition signal, a single letter of the alphabet, down towards the big ship. The answer came back promptly—a burst of anti-aircraft fire.[10]

As Lieutenant Hap Simpson watched from his nearby Dauntless, Sailer then picked up his map case and flipped through his booklet of enemy ship identification information. He found a matching silhouette, called Henderson Field on the voice radio, and reported the ship as a Japanese battleship of the *Kongo* class.[11] As it turned out, this was the battleship *Hiei*, one of the two that had been slated to shell Henderson Field with its eight mighty fourteen-inch guns. This was a formidable fighting vessel, long and sleek, with a top speed of nearly thirty knots. One year before, it had been one of only seven ships able to make the passage from Japan to Pearl Harbor without refueling.[12] The presence of this powerful ship so close to the island still posed a dangerous threat to the field, even in its damaged state.[13]

The dive-bombers and torpedo planes of Henderson Field, as well as planes from the *Enterprise* and elsewhere, lost no time in going after the *Hiei*; their attacks were launched as quickly and as continuously as possible. The first attack, leaving Guadalcanal shortly after six in the morning, came from five SBDs of the newly arrived VMSB-142, led by Major Robert H. Richard, which got one direct hit on the huge ship and one near miss. An hour later, Captain George Dooley of VMSB-131 led an attack with four TBF Avenger torpedo planes. This flight, in what one author has called the first torpedo attack ever delivered by Marine aviators,[14] got one hit on the ship. Then, at about eight-thirty, Sailer led an attack group of seven SBDs. This flight was supposed to be coordinated with the attack by Dooley's TBFs, but the action got too intense to maintain coordination. In any event, the Dauntlesses failed to get any hits on this flight.

The Henderson Field dive-bombers were not giving up. Later in the morning, after the planes of VT-10 had put three more torpedoes into the *Hiei*, Sailer led another Dauntless attack, this time with Robertshaw, Kollman, and Janson, and two pilots from other squadrons. The anti-aircraft fire coming from the battleship and its escorts was fierce, but the American pilots persevered, and Sailer, Kollman, and one pilot from another squadron connected with their 1,000-pound bombs on the battleship. The Cactus Air Force did not let up against this monstrous floating threat; Lieutenant McEniry led still another attack with seven other pilots, but bad weather spoiled their chance to hit the target. The pilots of VT-10 then put another three torpedoes into the ship. Finally, in the last attack before darkness closed down flight operations, Sailer led his fourth flight of the day. Accompanied by Robertshaw, Lieutenant Robert E. Kelly, and Gordon from his own squadron, and by four pilots from VMSB-141, he led one more assault on the dying battleship. Because of the extremely bad weather conditions at this point, Sailer was the only one to find the target. He managed to release his bomb and scored a direct hit or a near miss on a light cruiser that was serving in the screening force for the *Hiei*. The next day, the battleship had disappeared. The Marines later learned that the Japanese had abandoned and sunk her during the night. This was the first battleship sunk by the United States during the war.

On the 14th, the battle continued at its hectic pace. In the very early morning hours after midnight, Japanese ships rained eight-inch artillery shells down on the vicinity of Henderson Field for an hour or so. Hap Simpson described this type of shelling as "the most horrible thing a fellow can go through. . . . You just sit in your foxhole and tremble."[15] On this occasion, the bombardment caused consternation and lack of sleep for pilots already exhausted from the day's action, but little physical damage, largely because of the setbacks already suffered by the Japanese navy, which had few ships available to carry out the shelling. In the morning, Simpson went out to examine the crater left by a dud shell that had fallen about fifty feet from his foxhole. The shell, probably a fourteen-inch one, had "left a hole big enough for a man to crawl into, which I did. I remember I got into it up to the skull of my head."[16]

The Henderson Field flyers propelled themselves back into the fray before dawn. Sailer chose Charlie Kollman, known as the best dive-bomber pilot in the squadron after Sailer himself, and Hap Simpson to go up with him at first light, without bombs, to assess the results of the naval battle they had heard raging during the night. They fanned out to survey the waters surrounding Guadalcanal in order to determine the targets to be concentrated on. At various locations, they spotted numerous destroyers, several cruisers, one carrier, and one battleship. As Hap Simpson later put it, "Needless to say, we were most disappointed that we had no bombs when we flew over the enemy battleship."[17]

It soon became apparent that this was the all-out, last-ditch effort by the Japanese to invade and control Guadalcanal, and the Cactus Air Force was fully mobilized to meet the threat.[18] Sailer led the first attack of the day at about 6:30 in the morning, accompanied by Robertshaw, Kelly, Bright, McEniry, and Lieutenant John Skinner, with six F4F fighters as protection. Their target was a group about 170 miles away of four heavy cruisers and three destroyers, which were believed to have participated in the shelling of Henderson Field during the night. McEniry gives a detailed account of this attack in his book. Sailer led the dive-bombers down against a heavy cruiser of the *Atago* class, which, according to John Lundstrom, was the *Kinugasa*. Sailer released his bomb for a direct hit on the bow of the ship; Kelly got a direct hit on the bridge; McEniry, Bright, and Skinner all got near misses. According to Lundstrom, who has expertly analyzed Japanese reports of the battle, one of these bombs blew out large areas of the hull and killed the captain and his executive officer. The ship was beset with fires, flooding, and, soon, a ten-degree list. Meanwhile, Captain Dooley of VMSB-131 pressed the attack with his group of six torpedo planes, which put three or four torpedoes into a heavy cruiser.

Back at Henderson Field, according to Hap Simpson, the "big shots were running around, pulling their hair and yelling orders. We would go up and drop a bomb on them, then come back and get another one, and go back again." When McEniry and Sailer landed back at Henderson, Sailer said to him, "Mac, you didn't quite get a hit. Let's try again." The major then scratched out the names of the first two pilots scheduled for the next attack, and put down his own and McEniry's.[19] This time, the target was a convoy of eleven troop transports, screened by a large force of Japanese warships, steaming towards Guadalcanal with an invasion force. The transports, which were armed with a number of 13mm anti-aircraft machine guns, carried some 7,000 troops, tons of ammunition and supplies, and more than eighty landing craft.[20]

This was a major target indeed, and the Cactus Air Force, in coordination with the Navy planes and others, was directed to throw everything available at the approaching ships. The Navy and Marine commanders ordered constant flights; every plane that could fly was sent out to attack, return to re-arm, and go out again. The day was a hectic, blurred series of continuous attacks with no time to stop and think between flights. On Sailer's second mission of the day, he led seven other pilots from VMSB-132 and two from VMSB-142 in conjunction with nine SBDs and seven TBFs from other squadrons, escorted by eight Marine F4F fighters and four Army P-39 fighters.[21] They arrived over the convoy, which was arranged in three groups of transports, four or five to a group. McEniry said that this was "the largest convoy of ships any of us had ever seen."[22] Between the transports and the escorting warships, McEniry in his diary reported that a total of twenty-eight Japanese ships lay spread out below the dive-bombers.

Sailer's group attacked from the right side of the enemy formation, choosing two 8,000-ton transports as targets. According to the war diary of VMSB-132, Sailer's squadron, pressing on through a hail of heavy anti-aircraft fire and fending off determined opposition by enemy fighters, scored two hits on one of the transports, by McEniry and Herlihy; and three hits on the other, by Robertshaw, Kollman, and Gordon. A pilot from another Scout Bomber squadron (VMSB-142) got a fourth hit on the second ship.[23] In his book, though, McEniry says his bomb missed on this second attack, and that, when they landed, Sailer again went through his "Let's try again" routine, and replaced the first two names on the next attack roster with his and McEniry's.[24]

Sailer led the squadron's third attack of this day of unceasing flights, with Robertshaw, Herlihy, Kollman, McEniry, Simpson, Kelly, Skinner, and Gordon. They went out after the same group of transports they had attacked that morning, but, as McEniry put it, they found the ships in "disarray," as the destroyers moved through the formation of transports laying down smokescreens.[25] This time, again in the face of heavy anti-aircraft fire from the ships and opposition from fighters, Sailer and Herlihy both scored direct hits with their bombs on one transport, and three other pilots scored hits on other ships. Now, after suffering the last two misses, McEniry did everything in his power to ensure that he got a hit, and he succeeded. The result, when they got back to the field, was that Sailer said, "You got a beautiful hit, Mac. Now that we know how, let's go again."[26] So Sailer once more erased the top two names on the scheduling board, and he and McEniry went out on the fourth mission of the day. It is not clear from the war diary of VMSB-132 just who went on this last flight; McEniry clearly recalls that he got a near-miss on a destroyer and barely made it back to Henderson Field with his SBD badly shot up; there is no record of Sailer's activity on this mission, other than an entry in his log book showing that his fourth flight was an attack of 1.6 hours' duration.

There was another aspect of this string of successful missions, though, that tempered whatever exhilaration the pilots and their gunners felt. Hap Simpson recorded the feeling in his diary: "We sank many of their ships that day, and it certainly looked good to see them sinking and burning. However, not too good, because we would get down real low on our dive, and we could actually see them, the men on the troop ships. They must have packed them on these ships. . . ."[27]

On November 15, Sailer was airborne before six in the morning, leading a group of pilots from his squadron and VMSB-142. This time they were after four Japanese troop transports that were beached west of Kokumbona. In a flight lasting less than an hour, Sailer scored a hit, as did Wallof and Skinner. Sailer then led his second and last attack of the day, and of the big battle, with pilots from his squadron and VMSB-141. Again, Sailer scored a hit on a transport, as did Herlihy. They also strafed the Japanese landing positions with their .50-caliber machine guns.

With the end of the frantic battle of mid-November, Joe Sailer's greatest accomplishments at Guadalcanal were done. His squadron, in coordination with the other land-based and carrier-based dive-bombers and torpedo-bombers, as well as many other American units on the sea and in the air (not to mention the Marines on the ground, who still were battling sporadically with the increasingly desperate Japanese in the jungles of the island), had repelled the last enemy push to overwhelm the defenses of the crucial island. Although the war was to continue for nearly three years, many commentators mark the end of the Naval Battle of Guadalcanal on November 15, 1942, as a significant turning point in the course of the Pacific war; after that defeat, the Japanese lost their momentum, and were on the defensive from that time on.

Of course, although the men at Henderson field undoubtedly were aware of the great significance of their efforts in thwarting the desperate push of the invasion forces, the war and its hazards continued with just as much danger and uncertainty as before. The pace was less frenzied, but each separate mission was still fraught with hazards and threats from the enemy, the elements, and random accident. On November 17, with the big sea battle behind them, Sailer and Kollman were sent up on a special mission to bomb a Japanese ground position near Lambeti Plantation on Kolumbangara Island, to the west beyond New Georgia. This mission was unsuccessful in all respects; Kollman's bomb missed the target, and Sailer's bomb was a dud that failed to explode.

Sailer's next activity was on November 23, when he again led a group of pilots on a mission to attack Japanese positions on Lambeti Plantation.[28] This time they succeeded in bombing and strafing enemy buildings and starting small fires in the encampment.[29] Also on this date, the routine was lightened somewhat for the SBD squadrons when a new squadron, Navy Scouting 4, arrived to take over the anti-submarine patrols that the Marine flyers had been handling.

On November 25, Sailer went out on a special observation mission, flying for the first time at Guadalcanal with a rear-seat companion other than his regular radio-gunner, Howard Stanley.[30] Sailer reported seeing fires in the woods and gun flashes during the three-hour flight, but no other activity took place. On November 27, he led five of his pilots and three torpedo pilots on a mission after dark to find and attack three destroyers and two transports that were unloading troops on Munda, a small island in the New Georgia group. Three of the pilots were unable to locate Sailer for the rendezvous, and so returned to Henderson Field. In any event, conditions were not favorable for the attack; the moon was obscured by clouds, placing the targets in darkness. Sailer set off two flares at 2,000 feet above the water, but they were of little use. He made one exploratory dive to try to locate a target, but when he went back down on an attack dive, his bomb failed to release. His frustration mounted as he tried again with a third dive, but the bomb still would not fall. Ultimately, by the end of a four-and-one-half-hour flight, one of the dive-bomber pilots, Lieutenant Skinner, managed to get a single hit on the bow of a transport.

On November 28, Sailer was sent on a special mission to attack a submarine that had been sighted in the vicinity. He could not locate the sub, so he bombed enemy ground positions on Guadalcanal. On December 1, he led an attack group with eight other pilots to locate one light cruiser and two destroyers. They could not locate the ships after three hours of searching, and, after darkness fell, they headed home still carrying their bombs. A night landing carrying a thousand-pound bomb was not an ordinary event, and on this occasion the result was disastrous. As McEniry recounts in his book, Lieutenant Simpson landed first with his landing gear retracted, so his bomb was dragged along the metal-faced runway, with sparks flying.[31] Far worse was the result for Captain William F. Spang, who was making his first night landing in an SBD. His plane crashed into trees at the end of the runway, and he was killed.

On December 4, Sailer led an attack with six other pilots on four destroyers, but the weather made the visibility so bad that they could not locate the ships. On December 5, he led a special search to find reported enemy freighters, but again the searchers came up empty. Then, on December 6, according to one account, Sailer took a short flight that amounted to his "first vacation" since he assumed command of the squadron back in San Diego.[32] He flew a Grumman J2F float biplane to the nearby Auka Harbor, did some searching from the air, landed and had lunch with some "friendly natives," and returned the same day to Henderson Field with the plane's one big pontoon full of fresh pineapples.[33]

At some point in this period Sailer was given word of the new assignment he had dreaded—he was selected to become the new executive officer to Colonel William J. Fox, the commander of Henderson Field, which had been designated a Marine Corps air base on November 15.[34] This assignment was an important one, as he would have responsibility for supervising the operations of the airfield. However, this would not have been a tactical job, and would not have involved directing the flights or coordinating the attacks of his or any other squadron.[35] And, of course, it would not have involved any flying on his part. As he had told his mother in a letter months earlier from San Diego, the last thing he wanted was a staff job; he wanted to keep flying, and to keep leading the squadron he had worked with so diligently. Orders were orders, though, and he told his loyal rear-seat gunner, Howard Stanley, that they both would be grounded from now on—Sailer had a new job, and he didn't want Stanley to fly with anyone else.[36]

But the thought of giving up flying with his men evidently kept gnawing at him, and two officers who saw him at this time reported that he said he was going to see if he could get a reprieve from Brigadier General Roy Geiger, the Marine Corps aviation chief, who now was stationed far from Guadalcanal at the First Marine Air Wing headquarters on Espiritu Santo but was flying back for a brief visit.[37] During this visit Major General A.A. Vandegrift, commander of the First Marine Division, may have been scheduled to award a Japanese sword to Sailer.[38] So, in his own mind, Sailer may have felt the assignment was not yet final, because he would be talking to the general soon.[39] It also seems certain that he felt a strong urge to have one more shot at hitting a destroyer. He had never yet hit one of these speedy, elusive, relatively small targets, and his perfectionist side undoubtedly nagged at him to take this opportunity that fate had served up. There were destroyers out there; he hadn't yet started his new job; he could lead his men one last time and chalk up a destroyer before giving up the cockpit for a desk.[40]

In any event, on Monday, December 7, he clearly had been relieved as commander of the squadron. According to one account, he actually tried to report to the Guadalcanal aviation chief, General Louis Woods, on that day to begin his new duties, but was unable to see the general.[41] That afternoon, the Coastwatchers reported a force of eleven

enemy destroyers about 200 miles out, and a flight of thirteen SBDs was readied for the attack. Sailer and a lieutenant had been down at the Lunga River washing their
clothes; they were just returning from the river when
Howard Stanley met them and mentioned that a flight was
being formed to go out after the destroyers.[42] Sailer had little time to react to this news, and he did so instantly. Major
Robertshaw, now assuming command of the squadron,
was in the midst of conducting the briefing for the flight
when Sailer came into the operations shack and
announced that he would lead this one last attack. He
again went through the routine he had performed with
McEniry in November, this time crossing out Robertshaw's
name and substituting his own.

Sailer had grounded Stanley, and at this point he
made no effort to pull Stanley along on this flight. Instead,
he opted to take whatever gunner was available. As it
turned out, the man selected was James Woodward
Alexander, a twenty-year-old Marine private first class
from Los Angeles who had enlisted just after Pearl Harbor,
on January 2, 1942.[43] He had completed radio school, but
apparently not radio-gunner school, and had served with a
transport squadron, VMJ-152.[44] In December 1942, though,
he was not assigned to any flying or combat squadron, but
to a headquarters squadron of Marine Air Group 14. This
was to be Sailer's only combat mission without his regular
gunner, who had flown with him twenty-four times at
Guadalcanal.

Preparations for the mission were completed, and the
pilots readied their planes for takeoff. Just before Sailer
rolled his SBD down the runway, Navy Lieutenant William
Shields, who was detailed to the squadron as an intelli-

gence officer, took some late information from the operations officer out to the squadron leader's plane. Shields was the last person to talk to Sailer on the ground.[45]

The major led a three-plane section with Lieutenants Simpson and Donald Herrick; Kollman led another section with McEniry and Wallof. Also in the flight were Lieutenants E.P. McBryde and Frank Christian, and Lieutenant Pool and three other pilots from VMSB-142. The SBDs took off from Henderson Field at about 5:20 in the afternoon and rendezvoused with four F4F fighters over Savo Island. They headed up the Slot and at sunset, shortly after 6:30, located the group of eleven destroyers "of the new, large type" arrayed in columns of six and five.[46] The location was off North Bay, New Georgia, about 160 miles from Henderson Field. The American fighter planes stayed up at 11,000 feet, looking for enemy Zeroes or any other aerial menace that could interfere with the dive-bombers' mission. The Japanese, meanwhile, had deployed eight float biplanes, Mitsubishi F1M1s, code-named "Petes" by the Americans.[47] These were primarily designed for reconnaissance, but were used in tactical combat roles from time to time. They could carry bombs and were armed with three 7.7-millimeter machine guns.[48]

The destroyers began to maneuver violently and throw up a screen of anti-aircraft fire once the dive-bombers appeared. Sailer led his section down on the port column of ships through the hail of anti-aircraft fire. He executed a normal dive and released his bomb in a near miss that "caused the ship to rise in the water perceptibly."[49] Lieutenant Simpson, who was following him down on the ship, noticed that something was wrong—he came down behind the major, but passed him by. For some reason, Sailer's plane was going slowly as it came out of the dive and leveled off at 1,000 feet. Simpson cut his throttle and did an S-turn to look back to check. Sailer explained the situation, announcing calmly on the radio to all planes in the attack group that his dive flaps wouldn't retract. They appeared to be stuck, and he was going to try for a water landing at the southern end of New Georgia Island. This would be the logical response to this situation, because, with dive flaps stuck open, the SBD would not maintain level flight faster than about eighty-five or ninety knots, and he could not make it back to Henderson Field.

Then, as Simpson watched in horror, one of the Japanese Petes bore down on Sailer's plane from behind and above. Simpson and the others turned back to help, but they were too far ahead to get back in time. The biplane came up very close to the major's SBD and strafed it with its machine guns "from tail to nose."[50] Sailer's plane immediately rolled over. It "plunged head on into the sea and sank immediately."[51] The SBD pilots made some attempts to go after the attacking Pete and others in the area, but they got away. The F4Fs had remained at 11,000 feet throughout the attack, evidently never realizing that enemy float planes were present. As the mission continued, the other SBDs managed to get three hits on three destroyers. Several other pilots also were attacked by the Petes, and Herrick was wounded in the leg by machine-gun fire.[52] He and the other pilots returned safely to Henderson Field, however, leaving only their commanding officer and his gunner behind.

CHAPTER SEVEN
AFTERMATH

The immediate official reaction to Sailer's loss was expressed in after-action reports such as that of MAG-14:

In the death of Major Sailer, the flying forces of this country have lost one of their most outstanding, courageous, able and industrious officers. As CO of VMSB-132 he has participated in 25 missions from Henderson Field since November 1st; 19 of these were attack missions and on the twelve of these whereon contact was made with the enemy, Major Sailer scored 6 direct hits and 3 close misses. During the period from November 13–15, Major Sailer first contacted the Jap BB of the Kongo class early on the morning of the 13th off Savo Island, scored a direct hit on it later in the day, and another in a solo attack at dusk on a CL acting as part of its screening force. Early on the morning of the 14th he scored a direct hit on a CA of the Nachi class off New Georgia which later sank, and made 3 hits out of 4 attacks on the APs approaching Cactus on the 14th and 15th. The intangible effect of his leadership and person-

ality upon both officers and men in this period is
incalculable.[1]

The individual pilots had their own reactions. Hap
Simpson in his diary called the loss of his squadron leader
"quite a tragedy for us."[2] John McEniry later recalled that
the pilots "all felt a real sense of loss."[3] The squadron, of
course, continued on its missions under Major
Robertshaw, who was a very able flight leader and commanding officer. As events turned out, though, the period
of greatest crisis had passed, and the time soon came for
VMSB-132 to be rotated off Guadalcanal. By the end of
December, the remaining pilots had departed.

Back in the United States, it took a considerable time
for the bad news to reach home. In April of 1942 Sailer's
mother had moved out of the family's longtime home at
1718 Spruce Street in center-city Philadelphia, and had
taken up her solitary residence in the suburban neighbor-
hood of Chestnut Hill, out beyond Spring Bank, in a small
house at 8012 Crefeld Street. She had a great deal of interest in the war, with Joe in the Pacific and John, a Navy
lieutenant, stationed in Alaska. In addition, her four sons-
in-law were serving in the military in various capacities.

Not much news of Joe had reached her; the only word
she had received since his last letter from San Diego in
early October had been an official Marine postcard she had
received in mid-November advising her that he had been
transferred overseas. Finally, on November 28, she got definite word of his activities—through the newspapers. On
that day, the Philadelphia *Evening Bulletin* carried a
lengthy dispatch from Ira Wolfert, giving a delayed
account of the Naval Battle of Guadalcanal of November

12–15. Accompanying this long dispatch the paper ran a story with the local angle, headlined "Major Sailer's Squadron Helped Put Finishing Touches to Jap Battleship," and accompanied by a photograph of Joe. The article gave an account of his squadron's role in sinking the *Hiei*, along with the Navy and Marine torpedo planes. The paper reported that his mother "was immensely pleased when she learned of her son's accomplishment," but also quoted her as saying, "Joe is rather retiring . . . but he would be the first to insist that everyone who had part in the sinking be given credit."[4]

Sailer's relatives got further word of him in the November 29 edition of *The New York Times*, which ran a long, censor-delayed dispatch by Foster Hailey on "the Sea Fight That Finally Broke Attack on Guadalcanal," again giving details of the mid-November sea battle. In describing the attacks on the *Hiei*, the story related that

> Major Joe Sailer . . . who was so sore after two misses he would hardly talk to the Colonel [Albert D. Cooley], came back from his third dive on the Jap with a broad grin on his face.
>
> "I put one right amidship," he said, "throwing stuff in the air 500 feet."
>
> The other pilots knowing how keenly Sailer had felt his previous misses crowded around and slapped his back and told him, "Nice going, Joe."[5]

The media spotlight continued to shine on the local hero. On November 30, a somewhat less staid journal, the *Philadelphia Daily News*, presented an overview of the battle headlined "Shot-by-shot yarn of how our Navy pulped Jap fleet." Accompanying this account was the local angle in a separate story, with a photograph of Sailer: "Jap battleship sunk by Chestnut Hill ace." This story portrayed Mrs. Sailer as quite pleased at the news she heard: "It looks as if he isn't wasting much time." The reporter also managed to interview Sailer's niece, Emily Churchman, who evidently was visiting her grandmother: "This personal message to 'Uncle Joe' from his niece, Emmy, a little sweetheart, if there ever was one: 'Tell him to get another one for me' the laughing little blond urged."[6]

There was at least one more clear burst of good news in the press before the harsh reality caught up with the family. On December 9, the *Evening Bulletin* ran an update on the mid-November battle, headlined "Major Sailer Aided in Convoy Rout," and describing how Sailer and his squadron had helped account for not just one battleship, but "12 transports, loaded with 45,000 men of a task force aimed at retaking Guadalcanal."[7]

Press reports after that point brought other news of fighting in the Solomon Islands, but none, apparently, relating directly to Sailer.[8] Then, on December 26, 1942, perhaps timed to let her celebrate Christmas Day in peace, the Marine Corps sent Mrs. Sailer a telegram from Lieutenant General Thomas Holcomb, the Commandant of the Marine Corps:

DEEPLY REGRET TO INFORM YOU THAT YOUR SON MAJOR JOSEPH SAILER JR USMC HAS BEEN REPORTED MISSING IN ACTION IN THE PERFORMANCE OF HIS DUTY AND IN THE SERVICE OF HIS COUNTRY THE COMMANDANT APPRECIATES YOUR GREAT

ANXIETY AND WILL FURNISH YOU FURTHER
INFORMATION PROMPTLY WHEN RECEIVED
TO PREVENT POSSIBLE AID TO OUR ENEMIES
PLEASE DO NOT DIVULGE THE NAME OF HIS
SHIP OR STATION

There is no letter or other direct record available to describe the reaction of Joe Sailer's mother upon receiving this telegram. There is no doubt, however, that she was devastated by the thought of losing him, and for quite some time she did not accept the fact of his loss. She was to some extent encouraged in her lingering hope by some of the many statements that reached her over the next few weeks. Her friend Mrs. Newhall, who had connections in the military, wrote from San Diego on January 15, reporting that Sailer had been shot down, and saying she supposed "there is still some chance" he would return safely.[9] Major Robertshaw wrote her on January 19, saying "I am sorry that I can not report that he has been found as yet. We have not given up hope and you must not either."[10] He went on to say: "It is my duty to try to fill Joe's shoes as squadron commander until he comes back." Although her letter in reply does not survive, it evidently showed that she seemed to be beginning to accept her son's fate. Major Robertshaw wrote to his parents on February 14: "Mrs. Sailer got my letter, and I intend to write again one of these days. There is so little hope for her that I hesitate to give her any. I think she knows that, from her letter, but she can really take it. I guess she knows he is still living somewhere."

She was not to be left in doubt as to her son's fate for much longer, at least officially. In what may have been taken as a strong indication of the official view of the matter, the Marine Corps notified her on March 2 that Major Sailer would be awarded the Navy Cross "for extraordinary heroism in action . . . from November 10 to 15, 1942."[11] Before that medal was officially awarded, she received on April 1, 1943, the final telegram from the commandant, slightly garbled by the typist:

> DEEPLY REGRET TO INFORM YOU THAT YOUR SON JOSEPH MAJOR JOSEPH SAILER JR. U.S.M.C. NOW REPORTED KILLED IN ACTION IN THE PERFORMANCE OF HIS DUTY AND IN THE SERVICE OF HIS COUNTRY INSTEAD OF MISSING IN ACTION AS WAS PREVIOUSLY REPORTED TO PREVENT POSSIBLE AID TO OUR ENEMIES PLEASE DO NOT DIVULGE THE NAME OF HIS SHIP OR STATION REMAINS NOT RECOVERED PLEASE ACCEPT MY HEARTFELT SYMPATHY LETTER FOLLOWS

A letter did follow, in which the commandant expressed his "profound regret" at the death of Major Sailer.[12]

It seems fairly certain that, even after receiving these definite reports of his death, Mrs. Sailer did not accept that verdict as a fact. Undoubtedly at her urging, on April 7 her daughter Alice's husband, Lawrence Litchfield, wrote to Marine Corps headquarters inquiring about the change in Sailer's status from missing to killed. In about a week he received a reply, explaining that, although "missing" status usually is carried for one year, that status can be changed at any time on receipt of "information definite enough to cause a change in status to be made." The letter said that the change in this case was made "on the strength of a report recently received, which showed that he was shot down in action December 7, 1942, just after pulling out of a bombing dive."[13]

In an exchange of letters in mid-April with Sailer's old friend from San Diego, Martin Severson, now a major at Marine Corps headquarters in Washington, Mrs. Sailer evidently asked what could have happened to change Sailer's status so quickly. Severson replied:

> As soon as I reached Washington, I inquired through the casualty section about Joe. He was carried as missing then. However now I understand that information in squadron or group war diaries states that Joe was hit coming out of his dive, and that eyewitnesses saw him go down. I read the report of the group commander who paid a very glowing tribute to Joe, and he seemed convinced and sure that Joe was gone. I am being very frank and telling you exactly what I know.[14]

Yet Sailer's mother still was not ready to give up. Throughout her widowhood, from the end of 1928 until her death in 1963, she had never removed her wedding ring. On one occasion in her eighties when a jeweler asked her to remove the ring, she snapped at him in dismay, telling him that this ring would never leave her finger under any circumstances. Now, in the face of a series of authoritative reports of Sailer's death, she was not ready to leave him to that fate. She may have known that the chances of survival were fairly good for those pilots who survived the initial downing. Quite a few were rescued at Guadalcanal, some after having been missing for as long as twenty-six days.[15]

Mrs. Sailer received Joe's Navy Cross medal and citation in May.[16] She sent copies to various people, including Floy Larsen, the young woman who had stored Joe's automobile for him when he left Quantico for the West Coast in 1942. She also sent Floy some newspaper clippings, probably some about Joe's accomplishments, but also some that conveyed the message of desperate hope that Joe's mother still was clinging to. Floy replied: "Also want to thank you for the clippings. It is encouraging to read how one can be found after being missing so long & with so many odds against him."[17] Then, in July, Mrs. Sailer received a letter from Hilma Newman, who had been a friend of Joe's in Brooklyn when he worked for Sperry there, expressing her sympathy upon hearing of his death. Mrs. Sailer evidently sent back a very quick reply correcting Hilma's characterization of Joe's status, for Hilma sent another letter postmarked ten days after the first, saying "Thank you for your letter about Joe. Even though the chance of his return is so slim, some of the men who are shot down do live through incredible experiences. I hope Joe is in that group and will return one of these days."[18]

Acceptance gradually came over time, as it must. However, one more unfortunate report reached Mrs. Sailer, after passing through the distortions of the rumor mill. Floy Larsen, who was a fairly regular correspondent for a time after Joe's death, wrote Mrs. Sailer in June 1944 that she had met a combat correspondent for the Marine Corps, Jack de Chante (actually John A. DeChant, co-author of *Flying Leathernecks*), who told her that

Joe Foss (who had led the fighter planes on the same mission) told a Joe Renner that Joe got out of the plane OK, was in the water in a life belt, threw back his head and grinned, and waved to them. He said there were only land-based planes overhead, that they sent for others and when they arrived it was turning quite dark and they couldn't find Joe. Jack de Chante said he thought it was barely possible Joe might have been taken prisoner although it didn't appear very likely since those reports came in daily by radio.

I told Jack de Chante what Jack Cram had told me and how the stories differed but he seemed to be of the opinion that he had the correct details. . . . His description of Joe sounds so true to me and characteristic of Joe, I wonder if everyone else has told just what he feels is best for us to believe.[19]

There is no record of what emotional turmoil this mistaken report may have caused for Joe's family. In any event, the discrepancy was resolved within a few months. When DeChant's book, *Flying Leathernecks*, was published in October 1944, Floy immediately sent Mrs. Sailer a copy. Her letter did not mention the life belt story again, and DeChant, if he ever had thought Sailer was the one left afloat, did not repeat this error in the book. He (and his co-author, Richard G. Hubler) clearly reported Sailer's death[20] and reported the life belt incident in connection with the actual victim, Marine Lieutenant Colonel Harold W. Bauer, who was shot down November 14, 1942, in command of VMF-212, a squadron of F4F fighters. Foss and Renner saw him grinning in the water, and tried to rescue him, but could not find him after several tries.[21]

From about this time, Mrs. Sailer began to focus exclusively and diligently on preserving the many recollections of her son that poured in to her from those who knew him and had served with him. When *Flying Leathernecks* appeared, she bought a large number of copies and sent them to many of Joe's colleagues. This effort produced a number of responses expressing high opinions of his character and career. Even before she sent out the books, though, she had heard from a number of his military acquaintances. For example, Captain Charles Kollman, who had been with the squadron at Guadalcanal, wrote her in 1944 that her son "was one of the finest and most respected men I have ever known." He stated another opinion that was echoed by several others: "If you do not already know, Mrs. Sailer, your son did as much toward winning this war as any other one man."[22] Jack Cram, who went on to become a general, wrote her, also in 1944: "Joe is the outstanding Dive Bombing Pilot of the war."[23] Major Robertshaw, in his first letter to Mrs. Sailer after Joe was lost, wrote: "I can assure you that you can stand up with anyone and say that your son has done as much to win this war as any one man who has been in it thus far."[24]

Other accolades came from less-expected sources. Soon after Sailer was officially reported as killed in action, Mrs. Sailer received a letter from someone she did not know:

> You will no doubt be surprised to receive this letter. I am the mother of Staff Sergeant Robert E. Dougherty, Jr., who served under your son's command on Guadalcanal. We read so many times what commanding officers say of the men who served under them, that I thought I would

like to tell you what my son wrote of "our Major Joe" as he so affectionately called him. I will quote from his letter.

"I think I can tell you that Major Joe Sailer was C.O. of 132. A swell guy if I ever met one and it is a pleasure and an honor to be able to say I served under him. I will tell you all about him when I see you. As a skipper he was ace high and he rated the same as a man."

In speaking of the article in February Reader's Digest he also said "It mentioned 'our Major Joe' but didn't say near enough about him."

I'm sure Bob has no idea of my writing this but I know he won't mind, and I hope that you don't. With kindest regards and sincere sympathy,

I am,

Sincerely yours,

Anne F. Dougherty[25]

Then, in May 1943, just a few days after her son's Navy Cross was forwarded to her, Mrs. Sailer received a rather extraordinary letter from an official source within the Marine Corps:

20 May 1943.

My dear Mrs. Sailer:

Sometime ago I read the official report of the Group Commander of your son, Major Joseph Sailer. This report was confidential but it left no doubt in my mind but that Major Sailer had rendered one of the most outstanding services of any aviator in this war to date and for which unfortunately he made the supreme sacrifice. You have no doubt been advised about his citation but in case you have not I am sending you a copy of it. In my opinion, which I do not care to have quoted, his case warrants the Congressional Medal of Honor. It is one thing to sneak up on a Jap Zero and shoot it down with a burst of machine gun fire and after a few of such incidents be made an aviation ace but quite another to have "led six attacks in spite of intense aerial opposition and anti-aircraft fire, scoring direct hits on a Japanese battleship of the Kongo Class, a heavy cruiser, a destroyer and two transports."

I have been very anxious to communicate to you that information but did not feel at liberty to do so until it was released officially. My interest in the case is as Editor of the Marine Corps Gazette and as Historian of the Marine Corps. I intend to publish his picture and the citation together with any other pertinent information about his exploits in the June issue of the Gazette. If you have a good late photo of him I would like very much to borrow it as the only picture available to me is a very small official photograph which, however, for its size is very good.[26]

Sincerely yours,
C.H. METCALF
Colonel, U.S. Marine Corps

Of course, the awarding of medals is necessarily a somewhat subjective practice, and one person's Medal of Honor winner will merit the Navy Cross, or less, in another observer's view.[27] There is one objective statistic that seems to be of some significance, though: In the Second World War, eleven Marine Corps pilots were awarded the Congressional Medal of Honor; of these, ten were fighter pilots, and one was a dive-bomber pilot.[28]

Although he did not win the Medal of Honor, Sailer received many favorable mentions in published accounts during and after the war. However, when these accounts went beyond the objective facts to report on his personal demeanor or reactions to the war, they were not always accurate. Several factors contributed to these misperceptions. For one thing, Sailer was, as his mother told one newspaper reporter, rather "retiring," at least when on duty.[29] Jack Cram said that "[y]ou had to really know him to appreciate him."[30] The pilots who flew with him at Guadalcanal reported the same impression: He kept his feelings largely to himself.

Naturally, the published accounts often focused on the most dramatic episodes that Sailer was involved in, notably the sinking of the battleship *Hiei* on November 14. Ira Wolfert, a noted war correspondent who was on the scene in Guadalcanal, described this action and surrounding events of the Naval Battle of Guadalcanal in *The New York Times* on November 28 and 29, 1942. This same reporting appeared in condensed form in the *Reader's Digest* of February 1943.[31] This narrative appeared again in book form in January 1943, this time as part of an expanded account of the fighting in October and November.[32] Wolfert's was a straightforward account of the action, with no noticeable errors. Other reports were similarly matter-of-fact.[33]

Some authors, however, have gone somewhat too far in pursuit of colorful and dramatic prose. In *Flying Leather-*

necks, the book that Sailer's mother distributed widely to her family and to her son's military colleagues, the narrative focused more heavily on Sailer than did any other account written during the war. In their chapter entitled "The Men," the authors devoted eight full pages to a summary of his time at Henderson Field. For the most part, their reporting is accurate, drawing on official military records and some interviews with men who were at Guadalcanal. It errs in some small details, such as saying Sailer's family lived on the Main Line, rather than in Philadelphia itself,[34] and is misleading in reporting that "[a]fter graduating from Princeton, Sailer got a job with the Sperry Gyroscope Company in New York." That is literally true, but it was eight years after, with many other activities in between, notably his service in the Marine Corps Reserve and his work for United Air Lines.

Those errors of fact were minor. A more serious mistake was the book's statement, in recounting the events of his final flight, that "there was no gunner to accompany him."[35] But what really stood out in the minds of those readers of the book who knew Sailer, was the authors' description of his physical and mental condition at Guadalcanal—exhausted, distracted, obsessed:

> "I'm tired," Sailer mumbled again and again. He was due to lose more weight, to be even more tired before his tour of duty was done.
>
> The next day, his blue eyes sunken in his face and his clothes and hair dusty with the black sand of Henderson Field, Sailer and his men took off again.[36]

Earlier, the authors stated another recurring theme: "Joe Sailer had an obsession: he wanted, more than anything else, to sink a Jap destroyer."[37] And, in a general description, they portrayed him again as distracted: "He wore a continual air of abstraction, as though he had a special problem always on his mind."[38] They singled out his hair as a critical feature: "In a way, Sailer's hair symbolized his character and fate. It was clipped and bright like a helmet. He liked to wash it every day until it was blond as a halo, but he wasn't particularly vain about it."[39]

These descriptive passages, of course, were not designed to be precise factual statements; they were meant to convey the essential nature of Joe Sailer. Because *Flying Leathernecks* does not contain detailed notes on its sources, it is not possible to check the factual basis for all of these remarks. Based on the reactions of those who knew him, though, the book's picture of the human side of Sailer is not entirely accurate. After Mrs. Sailer sent him a copy of the book, Lieutenant Commander William Shields, one of the Navy intelligence officers attached to Sailer's squadron, thanked her for sending it, and then gave his candid reaction:

Naturally I feel very proud to have received the book from Joe Sailer's mother and shall treasure it for that reason as well as for its worth as the first authentic account of Marine aviation's part in the holding of Guadalcanal. As for the pages about Joe, I have read them three times now and feel that on the whole they have been successful in outlining what Joe meant to his squadron and the officers and men who came into contact with him. As one who swam in the Lunga with him and who interrogated him on many occasions the references to his hair, his air of abstraction and a desire to sink a destroyer seem to me far from the truth and much more devices of a person who, as you suggest, did not know Joe. Certainly no one on Guadal at that time had the clarity of thought and expression as to the administration of the field and the movements of the enemy to a greater degree than Joe. It was his undivided attention to all these problems at all times that impressed his associates. Rather than giving him an air of abstraction it gave him one of determination and of being "on the ball" consistently.

John Lawrence and I who served as his intelligence officers—Navy men were loaned to the Marines at that time for the purpose—had a great respect for Joe's imagination in thinking of improvements for operations or the living conditions of the squadron. He was the intelligence officer's dream in the stating of enemy dispositions simply and clearly.[40]

Jack Cram also received a copy of the book, and offered his criticisms to Joe's mother:

It [the book] is excellent, even though I feel that the write-up on Joe is way below par. Your observation that the authors did not really know him is correct. I knew both of the boys, Hubler and De Chant. They came in after Joe was in Guadalcanal and never knew him, actually. It's a shame and everyone's loss that they didn't.[41]

Major Robertshaw, evidently having received his copy later than others, also gave his impressions of the book to Mrs. Sailer:

> It is fairly accurate, too, but is dressed up to make it saleable. Hubert [sic], like all reporters, publicity men and correspondents dress up their copy with what they think the public wants to read. Joe never expressed any but the usual remarks that anyone expressed when they are tired. In fact, he complained less than anyone else.[42]

Others who knew him at Guadalcanal agreed that Sailer was not by any stretch of the imagination an impulsive character who acted under the spell of obsessions or whims. George Dooley, the torpedo squadron commander who had coordinated a crucial attack with Sailer's squadron in the mid-November battle, years later gave his assessment of his colleague's nature:

> [H]e was in complete control of himself. He respected what was going on and he wasn't foolhardy, but he wasn't frightened either. He was a tremendous leader and the guys all worshipped him.[43]

Overall, though, if taken with a grain of salt, the book's account of Sailer's service on Guadalcanal did not present too distorted a picture. The men who flew with him there agreed that the squadron commander was, to a certain extent, obsessed with getting a destroyer. Hap Simpson chose a more diplomatic term, calling Sailer's drive to attack one of those elusive ships a "keen desire."[44]

This passion could be explained rationally, though; Sailer was the kind of man who wanted to feel he could do his job thoroughly. Getting a destroyer was a part of that job, and it was a real challenge, as Simpson explained:

[T]hese were destroyers we went in on, and boy I'll tell you, they are hard to hit, because you see, they can turn on a dime compared with the bigger ships you know. They can turn so much and when you have to follow their turn, and when they change course and you're in a dive, it's awful difficult to do that and not put your plane in a skid which will throw your bomb off its target . . . very difficult to do.[45]

Major Robertshaw, years after the event, in speaking of Sailer's last flight, said the squadron leader was "very, very anxious to make the flight, because he wanted to be able to say he hit a destroyer. Not that that had anything to do with his ego," but he wanted to complete his record and have one last chance to fly as squadron commander. Sailer, the organized, dedicated skipper of the squadron, felt he had to be able to do everything his men and his squadron were called on to do. One of those things was to drop bombs on destroyers, so he was determined to prove himself capable of doing that part of the job. This was a rational "obsession," not one driven by ego or uncontrolled aggressive instinct.[46]

Sailer's regular gunner, Howard Stanley, who spent more time in combat with him than anyone else, had this perspective on the "obsession" theory:

References to Major Sailer's "obsession" with a bomb hit on a destroyer have been, in my opinion, exaggerated by a number of authors. The real reason he led the fatal flight was because he loved to lead his men and he knew that this would be his last opportunity to do so.

Major Robert Shaw [sic], the executive officer of VMSB-132, was a "Marine from the Old School"; a name given to marines who had served in China prior to the Japanese invasion. If I remember correctly, Robert Shaw had not been in Marine aviation very long before December 1941. He did not have as much experience piloting SBD's as most of our other pilots in the squadron. I feel this could also have been a reason for Major Sailer taking the last flight.[47]

Some accounts, however, unlike that in *Flying Leathernecks*, gave a more melodramatic picture of Sailer's combat career. An example of this approach is an article that appeared in *Aircraft Age* magazine in June 1944. Entitled "Major Sailer: Flying Leatherneck," appearing over the byline of a Marine Corps Reserve officer, the article was largely based on the account of Sailer's Guadalcanal service in *Flying Leathernecks*, but with a few colorful embellishments. A few excerpts convey the flavor of the narrative:

"Hell!" he snorted. "Perfect scores in practice and look what happens. There he was, sitting like a duck in a pond and I missed. Over anxious!"

Sailer scowled. "I'm going to get me a destroyer by God, if it takes all year." His voice was gritty with determination. . . .

That second miss put a kink into Joe Sailer's mind. He began to want a Jap destroyer. He wanted one worse than anything he had ever wanted before. It ate at him steadily. No medals, no heroics—just one Jap destroyer. . . .

Sailer's obsession about a destroyer burned in him. His displays of courage verged almost on the foolhardy. . . .

[On the day of his final flight, he said he would be coming along.] "Wait a minute, Joe," said one of his teammates, "You leave these babies to us. You don't have to go on this one!"

Sailer grinned and waved them away. "What do you think I am—superstitious?" he snorted. "Come on, let's get those dirty sons of baboons!"

Sailer scrambled into his SBD, not waiting for a rear-seat gunner. This was too good a chance to miss, and it was his last.[48]

Perhaps this article served as part of the inspiration for another bit of popular culture later that year. On Sunday, December 31, 1944, the *New York Herald Tribune* ran a color comic strip called "Fighting Marines," by Frank Tinsley, this edition featuring Major Joseph Sailer, USMC. Mrs. Sailer received copies in the mail from Floy Larsen and from Jane Watson, the sister of Thomas Watson of IBM and possibly the woman Sailer would have settled down with after the war. The strip really was just a single dramatic illustration of an SBD pulling up after a successful bombing run against a large ship, with one detailed caption running under the long, panoramic view:

One of the greatest dive-bomber pilots the Marine Corps ever had, "Skipper" Joe Sailer was noted for his reckless daring . . . Although he ran up a big score of Jap battle wagons, cruisers and even a carrier, Sailer had a yen to sink a Nip destroyer . . . At last his big chance came and he dove on the leader of a "tin can" flotilla. . . .[49]

Of course, this rather overblown and distorted account of Sailer's military accomplishments was a product of the war atmosphere. Some allowances should be made for the rather shrill and frenzied tone of the comic strip, and even for its errors of fact. The situation was to improve greatly in postwar years. There has been a rich profusion of books about Guadalcanal and related topics, such as the Cactus Air Force, the SBD in World War II, and Marine Corps aviation in general. A large number of these books contain accounts of Sailer's dive-bombing missions, and most of them present well-founded, factual descriptions, with only occasional errors, virtually none of them major.

By the end of 1944, Mrs. Sailer had settled into a state of resignation about the fate of her son. She maintained scrapbooks with every available clipping, photograph, and piece of correspondence that mentioned him. There were few new items to accumulate after the war ended. She had received his posthumous Navy Cross medal and citation in May 1943, and she continued to correspond with those who had known her son or knew of his accomplishments. In 1944, Colonel Clyde H. Metcalf, the editor of the *Marine Corps Gazette* who had earlier requested a photograph of Joe to include in the magazine, replied to a letter from his mother, providing his further assessment of Joe's career:

[I]t is universally considered by those who know that he stood for as much in the dive-bomber aviation field as Joe Foss and others stand for in the fighter plane field. When the full story of Marine Corps aviation in this war is written, I am sure that he will have a prominent place.[50]

In February 1945 Mrs. Sailer, her daughters Alice and Betty, and her son John traveled to the new Sperry plant in Great Neck, Long Island, for a tour and a showing of Sperry's 1942 film, "Experiences in England." The movie included some brief footage of Joe standing with Fred Vose, Joe smoking his pipe and smiling, and, although he was not clearly recognizable, controlling a gun turret inside a British bomber. The shots of Joe amounted to only a few seconds in total, because he did most of the cinematography himself.

It was not until September 1948 that the rest of Joe's medals were forwarded to her by the Marine Corps: the Presidential Unit Citation for the First Marine Division's service in the Solomon Islands and several others.[51] She kept up an exchange of Christmas cards and occasional letters with Howard Stanley until her death from cancer in 1963 at the age of eighty-eight.

CHAPTER EIGHT
FINAL THOUGHTS

In his book about the experiences of VMSB-132 at Guadalcanal, John McEniry asked the question that must have occurred to many of Joe Sailer's relatives, friends, and colleagues: Would it have made any difference if his regular gunner, Howard Stanley, had been with him on the December 7 flight?[1] Major Robertshaw, speaking many years after the fact as a retired general, did not hesitate in responding: "No, it wouldn't have made any difference, because his final problem was mechanical." In his view, once the airplane was slowed down by failure of the dive brakes to close, it was a "sitting duck." It was very difficult for even the best gunner to shoot down an attacking airplane, and there apparently were multiple float planes converging on the crippled Dauntless. Perhaps, he said, if there had been other SBDs or American fighters near enough to help that would have made a difference, but the rear guns in Sailer's own plane could not have made up for the lack of evading speed.[2] Howard Stanley was, understandably, still upset many years later at the turn of events on that December 7; he wondered if he shouldn't have kept quiet when he met Sailer on the way down to the river. Stanley realized, though, that Sailer would have found out about the sighting of the destroyers soon enough, and he inevitably would have gone out after them.[3]

There is little doubt that, despite the brief duration of his combat career, Sailer was one of the most successful American dive-bomber pilots of the war; he is credited by the official report of MAG-14 with flying nineteen combat missions and getting six direct hits and three close misses in the twelve missions on which the enemy was contacted.[4] The question is, what was the foundation of his success? There were several factors at work. First, he had a great deal more experience than most pilots, having begun his flight training in 1930, with intermittent flying ever since, and a great deal of flying from 1938 up to the start of the war, except for his several months in England in 1940 and 1941. Relatively few men had been trained during that period, because Marine Corps aviation was operating at a very limited level.

It was not just a question of extensive training, though. Sailer probably had the ideal nature for a combat pilot and leader. He was well-organized and meticulous in his approach to flying; he was a perfectionist who worked on his procedures until he got them down. By all accounts, it is no easy feat to pilot a bomber from high altitude through a sharp dive down through bursting anti-aircraft fire, sighting the target through a narrow tube, manning the machine guns, and preparing to operate a bomb release with precise timing. Sailer had practiced this procedure as effectively as could be done in peacetime, and he was meticulous in his execution. Where some pilots would release the bomb at a higher altitude to cut the risks, Sailer made sure he got down to the level of 1,500 to 2,000 feet where the bomb could hit with accuracy. In short, he was methodical, level-headed, and determined to get the job done right. Added to this mixture was either fearlessness or the ability to let duty override fear. When his dive flaps failed him on December 7, he showed his coolness under fire, announcing calmly and logically that he would try for a water landing off New Georgia.

Finally, it is fair to say that another factor contributing to Sailer's success was that, quite simply, he loved his work. Ever since he saw that little Waco biplane cavorting in the skies above Princeton, he wanted to seek his fortune behind the control stick of an airplane. He had a passion for flying, and that passion, coupled with his sense of duty and his inborn ability to get a job done thoroughly and effectively, enabled him to stand out for a few brief weeks as one of the outstanding combat pilots of the Pacific war. Perhaps even more important, his inner qualities helped him to inspire the men of his squadron to do the best job they possibly could in the face of the daunting conditions they faced in the early days of the crucial campaign for Guadalcanal.

APPENDIX A

NOTES ON THE FIRST OPERATIONAL BOMBING ATTACK WITH SPERRY O-1 BOMBSIGHT IN WORLD WAR II

Date: 30th April 1941

Aircraft: Lockheed Hudson Mk V, No T9340—220 Squadron, Coastal Command, Royal Air Force.

Duration of Mission: 6.05 hrs

Bombload: 4 x 250 GP, nose fused, 1 sec delay

Altitude: 8000ft (below cloudbase)

Target: 7/800 ton Armed Supply Ship

Location: Tyboron, Denmark—56°42'N 08°12'E

Crew: Captain: F/O J.D. Mallinson

Co-pilot: F/O J. Halstead

WOP/AG: Sgt Fawcett

" " Sgt Sutton (Wireless operator/Air gunners)

Wg Cdr Charles Dann, i/c Bomb Performance Test Squadron, Aircraft & Armament Experimental Establishment, RAF Boscombe Down

General Information: No: 220 Squardon [sic] was based at Thornaby, Yorkshire.

Crew was detached to A&AEE Boscombe Down on Air Ministry orders for special experimental trials. The attack was mounted from RAF Dyce, Scotland and aircraft returned to RAF Wick afterwards for debriefing and processing photos.

The bombsight was classified Secret to prevent the enemy from knowing of its use by the RAF. Strict orders were given that it must not fall into their hands and in the event of trouble the aircraft was to be ditched in deep water.

Several operational sorties were made from East Coast bases before the conditions were found in accordance with the above orders.

The crew then returned to A&AEE to assess the night attack potential. On 17th May, with full moonlight, an attack was launched from RAF Thorney Island, on south coast, against the Benz Works in Cherborg, France. This Works was located near a hospital hence the need for accuracy. The attack was made at 12,000ft using the reflection of the sea to pin-point the location. It was successful but there was very considerable enemy anti-aircraft fire and violent avoiding action had to be taken eventually landing us at RAF Manston on the eastern tip of England for debriefing before returning to Boscombe Down.

We eventually were recalled to squadron duties, Jimmy Halstead became crew captain and they were all lost during a low level shipping strike on 2 Aug 1941.

The Sperry O-1 was, unquestionably the most accurate bombsight used by the RAF. Had it been available earlier it would have saved many aircraft during the low level anti-shipping attacks. These ships were carrying vital strategic materials needed by the enemy and the vessels were heavily armed. The Nordern [sic] bombsight was not available for the RAF and I cannot comment on its alleged accuracy. The United States entered the War in the [sic] December and the whole aspect of precision bombing altered.

[signed] John S. Mallinson

APPENDIX B

A viators Flight Log Book Entries of Joseph Sailer Jr. at Guadalcanal

Nov. 1942

Date	Type of Machine	Duration of Flight	Character of Flight	Pilot	Passengers	Remarks
2	SBD-3	4.2	I	Sailer	Stanley	Observation
3	"	2.7	J	"	"	Search
5	"	4.6	J	"	"	"
7	"	2.2	G	"	"	Attack
8	"	4.1	J	"	"	Search
10	"	2.3	G	"	"	Attack
12	"	1.6	G	"	"	"
13	"	1.6	G	"	"	"
13	"	1.0	G	"	"	"
13	"	2.1	I	"	"	Observation
13	"	1.6	G	"	"	Attack
14	"	2.8	G	"	"	"
14	"	2.3	G	"	"	"
14	"	2.3	G	"	"	"
14	"	1.6	G	"	"	"

15	"	0.8	G	"	"	"
15	"	1.1	G	"	"	"
17	"	3.4	G	"	"	"
23	"	3.4	G	"	"	"
25	"	3.1	I	"	Ruffon	Observation
27	SBD-3	4.5	I	Sailer	Stanley	Observation
28	"	0.9	I	"	"	"

Dec. 1942

Date	Type of Machine	Duration of Flight	Character of Flight	Pilot	Passengers	Remarks
1	SBD-3	3.8	G	Sailer	Stanley	Attack
4	"	2.8	G	"	"	"
5	"	2.8	G	"	"	"
7	"		G	"	Alexander	"

APPENDIX C

THE SECRETARY OF THE NAVY
WASHINGTON
The President of the United States takes pleasure in presenting the NAVY CROSS to
MAJOR JOSEPH SAILER, JR., U.S. MARINE CORPS,
for service as set forth in the following
CITATION:

"For extraordinary heroism as a pilot of Marine Scout-Bombing Squadron ONE THIRTY-TWO in action against enemy Japanese forces in the Guadalcanal Area from November 10 to 15, 1942. Zealously seeking out and engaging the enemy under extremely hazardous conditions, Major Sailer led six attacks in spite of intense aerial opposition and anti-aircraft fire, scoring direct hits on a Japanese battleship of the Kongo Class, a heavy cruiser, a destroyer and two transports. His determined fighting spirit and unyielding devotion to duty contributed decisively to our success in routing the Japanese forces."

For the President,
[signed] Frank Knox
Secretary of the Navy.

NOTES

Chapter One

1. "Sale at Chestnut and 13th Streets Sets Price Record," *Philadelphia North American*, ca. 1916.
2. *Philadelphia North American*, April 12, 1886.
3. Undated manuscript entitled "Spring Bank," by John Welsh Young. The estate was the home of Edward Lowber, father of Mary Lowber Welsh, wife of John Welsh. John Welsh and his family stayed there during the summers.
4. Obituary of Joseph Sailer, *The New York Times*, Jan. 16, 1883.
5. "Hun Doctors Maltreated Many Yankee Prisoners, Declares Colonel Sailer," Philadelphia newspaper (unidentified), ca. Feb. 1919.
6. Joseph Sailer Jr. to Joseph Sailer Sr., ca. 1918. Joseph Sailer Jr. was not an accomplished speller; all quotations of his writings leave his spelling unchanged.
7. Alice Lingelbach, interview by author, Camden, Me., Aug. 1, 1994.
8. Mary Lowber Sailer to Joseph Sailer Sr., ca. 1918.
9. Edna St. Vincent Millay to Norma Millay, New York, June 20, 1917, *Letters of Edna St. Vincent Millay*, ed. Norma Millay (New York: Harper & Brothers, 1952), p. 67. The letter said, in part: "If I am at home I shall work very hard this summer, at something or other,—I have a perfect passion for earning money, don't care much how I earn it, just feel I have to hurry around all the time and make money."
10. The poem reads as follows:

141

My candle burns at both ends;
It will not last the night;
But ah, my foes, and oh, my friends
It gives a lovely light!

11. Endsley P. Fairman, telephone interview by author, tape recording, May 23, 1994.

12. Endsley P. Fairman, telephone interview by author, tape recording, May 25, 1994.

13. Dr. Charles Stephenson, telephone interview by author, tape recording, June 13, 1994.

14. Ibid.

15. Ibid.

16. Joseph Sailer Jr. to Joseph Sailer Sr., October 2, 1928.

17. Obituary, "Herbert Welsh, 89; Friend of Indians," *The New York Times*, June 30, 1941.

18. This accomplishment has not been verified. Miss Strawbridge's niece, Alice Lingelbach, repeated the story of this feat to the author in August 1994, but the family tradition adds the feature that Anne West Strawbridge was the first woman to climb the Matterhorn. This does not seem to be the case in a literal sense; it appears to be well-accepted that the first woman to scale the mountain was Lucy Walker, in 1871. Arnold Lunn, *Matterhorn Centenary* (New York: Rand McNally, 1965), p. 95. Perhaps Miss Strawbridge was the first Philadelphia woman to climb it.

19. The autogiro, which has long since faded from the world of aviation, originally was developed by a Spaniard, Juan de la Cierva, in the early 1920s. Harold Pitcairn later acquired the right to market the craft in the United States, where he advertised his model in alluring, illustrated brochures as a luxury item for the well-to-do, which could land on country estates and carry golfers to their matches. It was a Pitcairn model that Anne West Strawbridge bought, perhaps inspired by this advertising campaign. However, the autogiro was by no means easy to fly safely, and its inherent problems, coupled with the economic climate in the 1930s, eventually led to its demise. For a good summary of the history of the autogiro, see Warren R. Young, *The Helicopters, The Epic of Flight Series* (Chicago: Time-Life Books, 1982) pp. 51–67.

20. "Pilot Killed in 'Giro Crash at Hatboro," *Philadelphia Inquirer*, August 11, 1935.

21. Alice Lingelbach, interview by author, Camden, Me., August 1, 1994. Joseph Sailer Jr. reacted to the accident as follows in a letter to his mother:

> I was certainly sorry to hear about the terrible experience which Aunt went through. I can easily imagine how she must have felt, and although it appeared to be an accident which was absolutely uncalled for, I guess it was just one of those things which could not be helped.

Joseph Sailer Jr. to Mary Lowber Sailer, Aug. 22, 1935.

22. Joseph Sailer Jr. to Mary Lowber Sailer, July 1, 1936.

23. "Anne Strawbridge, Authoress, Is Dead," *Philadelphia Inquirer*, September 10, 1941.

Chapter Two

1. Joseph Sailer Jr. to Mary Lowber Sailer, June 18, 1930.

2. Ibid.

3. Ibid.

4. Ibid.

5. Joseph Sailer Jr. to Mary Lowber Sailer, July 15, 1930.

6. Joseph Sailer Jr. to Mary Lowber Sailer, ca. Feb. 1931.

7. Ibid.

8. Joseph Sailer Jr. to Mary Lowber Sailer, ca. 1931.

9. Joseph Sailer Jr. to Mary Sailer, Nov. 23, 1930.

10. Joseph Sailer Jr. to Mary Lowber Sailer, Feb. 14, 1931.

11. Diary of Joseph Sailer Jr., March 16, 1931. The full entry for the day is as follows:

> A disastrous morning in Corsairs. It was very bumpy. I was pilot for the 1st hr. & $1/2$ & Heist for the second hop. I had trouble with my first radio set & Heist came down & we got another one. For about $1/2$ hr. every thing went all right, but then I suddenly got very air-sick & had to heave over the side right in the middle of a long message. Godlove, Holsenbeck, Jenkins & Peterson all got sick also I heard when I came down. Played golf this afternoon & attended Marine lecture to-night.

12. Diary of Joseph Sailer Jr., March 13, 1931.

13. Diary of Joseph Sailer Jr., March 20, 1931.

14. Joseph Sailer Jr. to Mary Lowber Sailer, July 2, 1931.

15. Ibid.

16. Ibid.

17. Joseph Sailer Jr. to Mary Lowber Sailer, March 21, 1932.

18. Joseph Sailer Jr. to Mary Lowber Sailer, Oct. 25, 1931.

19. Diary of Joseph Sailer Jr., July 29, 1931.

20. Diary of Joseph Sailer Jr., July 30, 1931.

21. Joseph Sailer Jr. to Mary Lowber Sailer, April 8, 1932.

22. Joseph Sailer Jr. to Mary Lowber Sailer, April 28, 1932.

23. Ibid.

24. Joseph Sailer Jr. to Mary Lowber Sailer, June 28, 1932.

25. Edward C. Johnson, *Marine Corps Aviation: The Early Years 1912–1940*, History & Museums Division, Headquarters, United States Marine Corps, 1977, pp. 37–38 (quoting James Webb, one-time head of the National Aeronautics and Space Administration, who entered the reserves in the summer of 1930).

26. Joseph Sailer Jr. to Mary Lowber Sailer, March 21, 1932.

27. Joseph Sailer Jr. to Mary Sailer, Oct. 10, 1932.

28. Joseph Sailer Jr. to Mary Lowber Sailer, Dec. 24, 1933.

29. Joseph Sailer Jr. to Mary Sailer, May 22, 1934.

30. Joseph Sailer Jr. to Mary Lowber Sailer, July 24, 1934.

31. Ibid.

32. Charles Evans to Herbert Freuler, Feb. 11, 1936.

33. Joseph Sailer Jr. to Mary Lowber Sailer, Oct. 6, 1935.

34. Joseph Sailer Jr. to Mary Lowber Sailer, March 16, 1936.

35. Joseph Sailer Jr. to Mary Lowber Sailer, May 20, 1936.

36. Joseph Sailer Jr. to B.C. Voight, United Air Lines, Feb. 4, 1937.

37. B.C. Voight, United Air Lines, to Joseph Sailer Jr., Feb. 9, 1937.

38. Joseph Sailer Jr. to Mary Lowber Sailer, April 7, 1937.

39. Marion Crozer to Joseph Sailer Jr., June 16, 1937.

40. Horace S. Mazet letter to author, Jan. 20, 1995.

41. Joseph Sailer Jr. to Mary Lowber Sailer, April 2, 1938.

42. Joseph Sailer Jr. to Arthur R. Weckel, Sperry Gyroscope Co., Nov. 8, 1938.

43. *Current Biography Yearbook*, 1962, s.v. "Webb, James E(dwin)."

Chapter Three

1. Franklin Joseph, letter to author, March 28, 1994.
2. Hilma Newman to Mary Lowber Sailer, July 3, 1943.
3. Priscilla Wilson and Alice Lingelbach, interview with author, Camden, Me., Aug. 6, 1994.
4. Carl A. Frische, letter to author, Aug. 22, 1994.
5. *Encyclopedia Britannica*, 15th ed., s.v. "gyroscope."
6. *Encyclopedia Britannica*, 15th ed., s.v. "Sperry, Elmer Ambrose."
7. Philip A. St. John, *Bombardier: A History* (Paducah, Kentucky: Turner Publishing Co., 1993), p. 27.
8. Carl A. Frische, letter to author, Feb. 27, 1994.
9. Ibid.
10. Franklin Joseph, letter to author, March 28, 1994.
11. Arnold Hague, *Destroyers for Great Britain: A History of 50 Town Class Ships Transferred from the United States to Great Britain in 1940* (Annapolis: Naval Institute Press, 1990), pp. 7–10; Michael Gannon, *Operation Drumbeat: The Dramatic True Story of Germany's First U-Boat Attacks Along the American Coast in World War II* (New York: Harper & Row, 1990, reprint, New York: HarperPerennial, 1991), p. 83 (page citation is to the reprint edition).
12. Franklin Joseph, letter to author, March 28, 1994.
13. Joseph Sailer Jr. to Mary Lowber Sailer, Oct. 14, 1940.
14. Carl A. Frische, letter to author, Feb. 27, 1994.
15. Joseph Sailer Jr. to Mary Lowber Sailer, Oct. 14, 1940.
16. Franklin Joseph, letter to author, June 28, 1994.
17. Carl A. Frische, letter to author, Feb. 27, 1994.
18. John Keegan, *The Second World War* (New York: Penguin Books, 1990), p. 118.
19. Hague, *Destroyers for Great Britain*, pp. 14, 15, 60.
20. Joseph Sailer Jr. to Mary Lowber Sailer, Oct. 30, 1940.
21. Joseph Sailer Jr. to Mary Lowber Sailer, Nov. 2, 1940.
22. Ibid.
23. After her arrival in England, *Lincoln* did escort duty in the Eastern Atlantic until September 1941; she participated in one rescue operation in June. Thereafter she underwent a refit until March 1942, when she was assigned to the Royal Canadian Navy, manned by the

Royal Norwegian Navy. Later still she was re-assigned a British crew, and finally she was transferred yet again, in August 1944, to the Russians, and re-named *Druzhny*. She eventually was transferred back to Britain after the war, and was broken up for scrap metal in 1952. Hague, *Destroyers for Great Britain*, p. 60. The first donation to *Lincoln's* canteen fund was made by Joseph Sailer Jr., who received a cordial thank-you note from Lieutenant Brown, R.N., on behalf of the Canteen Committee, dated December 6, 1940.

24. Joseph Sailer Jr. to Mary Lowber Sailer, Nov. 18, 1940.
25. Ibid.
26. Franklin Joseph, letter to author, June 28, 1994.
27. Joseph Sailer Jr. to Mary Lowber Sailer, Dec. 10, 1940.
28. Joseph Sailer Jr. to Mary Lowber Sailer, Jan. 8, 1941.
29. Franklin Joseph, letter to author, May 2, 1994.
30. Franklin Joseph, *Letters Home from Britain at War* (New York: privately published, 1942), p. 16.
31. Franklin Joseph, letter to author, March 28, 1994.
32. Ivor Bowen, born in 1902, went on to a very distinguished career in aeronautics. After the war he held posts such as Chief Superintendent of the Aeroplane and Armament Experimental Establishment at Boscombe Down and Principal Director of Aircraft Equipment Research and Development in the Ministry of Supply. *Who's Who 1985*, s.v. "Bowen, Ivor." Bowen and Sailer did not get a chance to say goodbye in person when Sailer returned to the United States, and Bowen sent him a note dated May 13, 1941, through Franklin Joseph, expressing his appreciation for Sailer's work:

"All I can say now is that you have won the friendship & gratitude of all of us by the way you have worked for and with us and by your irresistible personality. . . .

"But you know, we in England are not given to flowery speeches, nor for that matter are you yourself, so when I say that I shall often think of you & look forward to the day when you can return you will know that I sincerely mean every word.

"There is so much to see—the road to Wolverhampton without rain and without darkness! London lit-up (in several ways)—a quiet English countryside without the shadow of war—all awaiting your revisit—& if on your honeymoon so much the better!

"And now the farewell which I missed saying in person—and I wish you the *very best* in your new career.

"With my personal thanks for all that you did."

33. *Experiences in England*, Sperry Gyroscope Corp., 16mm, 1942.
34. Joseph Sailer Jr. to Mary Lowber Sailer, Feb. 7, 1941.
35. Joseph, *Letters Home*, p. 17.
36. Franklin Joseph, letter to author, March 28, 1994.
37. Barry Taylor, *Pan American's Ocean Clippers* (Blue Ridge Summit, PA: Tab, 1991), pp. 5–6.
38. Diary of Trip to England, April 27, 1941, Major General H.H. Arnold, Arnold papers, Manuscript Room, Library of Congress.
39. In the classic movie *Casablanca* of 1942, the narrator explains at the outset that many of the people who frequented Rick's Cafe and other haunts in Casablanca were seeking desperately to find a way to get to Lisbon, and from there to the United States.
40. R.E.G. Davies, *Pan Am: An Airline and its Aircraft* (New York: Orion Books, 1987), pp. 42–43.
41. Taylor, *Ocean Clippers*, pp. 164–65.
42. Joseph, *Letters Home*, pp. 93–94. See also Arnold Diary, April 28–May 1, 1941.
43. The London *News Chronicle* for June 6, 1941, published two photographs of the results of this mission. One of the pictures was accompanied by the following text:

"The importance of this photograph is in the Air Ministry caption. Releasing the picture, the Ministry says that one salvo from a Hudson plane at 8,000 feet made a direct hit on this Nazi supply ship in Tyboron Harbour, Denmark, 'with the aid of the deadly new U.S. Sperry bomb sight.'

"This is the first official disclosure that the R.A.F. is using the famed Sperry sight, which was last year made available to Britain.

"The principal difference between this sight and the standard R.A.F. one appears to be that the R.A.F. apparatus is based on a telescopic sight requiring the alignment of cross hairs to fix the moment when the bomb should be released.

The pilot maneuvres the aircraft according to the orders of the bomb-aimer. The Sperry sight is understood to be built around the automatic gyroscopic pilot, which makes it possible for the bomb-aimer to control the aircraft himself while he is aiming at the target.

"Reports from America have stated that in tests remarkably accurate results have been obtained up to heights above 20,000 feet. America now has another automatic bomb sight— the Nordern [sic]—for which even greater accuracy is claimed."

Further details of this mission are set forth in a fact sheet prepared by the mission's commander, Flight Officer J.D. Mallinson, which is reproduced at Appendix B.

44. Carl A. Frische, letter to author, Aug. 4, 1994.

45. Wing Commander John Mallinson to Franklin Joseph, 1988. In this letter, Mallinson said:

"After the Tyboron raid we returned to Boscombe Down to assess the night attack potential. On the 17th of May, with full moonlight, the first night attack was launched from RAF Thorney Island, on the south coast, against the Benz Works in Cherborg, France. The Works was located near a hospital hence the need for accuracy. We were at 12,000 feet and used the reflection of the sea to pin-point the location. This was also a successful raid but there was very considerable enemy anti-aircraft fire and violent avoiding action had to be taken, eventually landing us at RAF Manston on the eastern tip off England for debriefing before returning to Boscombe Down."

46. Joseph, *Letters Home*, p. 74.

47. *Experiences in England*.

48. John D. Mallinson, "Notes on the first operational bombing attack with Sperry O-1 bombsight in Word War II," undated.

49. Arnold noted:

"I heard from British pilots stories of their unsuccessful attempts to do daylight bombing. One pilot who had been over Germany twenty-four times said it would be impossible for us to use our bombsight because of the heavy antiaircraft fire and the German fighter attacks. Bombers over German cities had to use continuous evasive action and could not fly in a straight level flight long enough for accurate sighting. That was my introduction to a general campaign that later developed into an official deprecation of our daylight bombing and a constantly nagging effort to get us to go along with the R.A.F. in their night bombing."

H.H. Arnold, *Global Mission* (reprint, Blue Ridge Summit, PA: Tab Books, Military Classics Series, 1989), pp. 215–16. Later in this discussion, he noted: "The British are not using the Sperry sight that we sent over." Ibid. at p. 225.

50. Franklin Joseph, letter to author, June 14, 1994.
51. Carl A. Frische, letter to author, Aug. 4, 1994.
52. For a general discussion of the controversy about the eventual adoption by the United States military forces of the Norden sight instead of the Sperry, see Loyd Searle, "The Bombsight War: Norden vs. Sperry," *IEEE Spectrum* (September 1989): pp. 60–64.

Chapter Four

1. This designation is interpreted as follows: the "V" stands for heavier-than-air (that is, airplanes rather than blimps); the "M" is for Marine; and the "SB" means Scout Bombers (that is, airplanes suited for bombing and for searching, or scouting, for enemy equipment and activities).
2. Joseph Sailer Jr. to Mary Lowber Sailer, July 4, 1941.
3. Joseph Sailer Jr. to Mary Lowber Sailer, Dec. 11, 1941.
4. Joseph Sailer Jr. to Mary Lowber Sailer, Jan. 10, 1942. Sailer was very intent on having his relatives enjoy the use of this marvelous new invention. He wrote his seven-year-old nephew soon after:

   If Granny has not already gotten the "Swim-fins" which were in may car, tell her to be sure to do so, because there is one pair that will just fit you & they will be lots of fun for swimming next summer. Also with the rubber shortage it is now impossible to buy any more.

   Joseph Sailer Jr. to William White Jr., January 21, 1942.
5. Joseph Sailer Jr. to William White Jr., April 26, 1942.

6. Joseph Sailer Jr. to Mary Lowber Sailer, March 13, 1942.

7. Ibid.

8. Edward Wallof, telephone interview with author, tape recording, June 13, 1994.

9. Joseph Sailer Jr. to Mary Lowber Sailer, April 1942.

10. Joseph Sailer Jr. to Mary Lowber Sailer, June 28, 1942.

11. Gordon W. Prange, *Miracle at Midway* (New York: McGraw-Hill, 1982; reprint, New York: Penguin Books, 1983), p. 74 (page citation is to the reprint edition).

12. Barrett Tillman, *The Dauntless Dive Bomber of World War II* (Annapolis: Naval Institute Press, 1976), pp. 4–16.

13. Tillman, *Dauntless Dive Bomber*, p. 12.

14. John Howard McEniry Jr., *A Marine Dive-Bomber Pilot at Guadalcanal* (Tuscaloosa: University of Alabama Press, 1987), pp. 114–15.

15. Franklin Joseph, letter to author, May 2, 1994.

16. Franklin Joseph, letter to author, June 14, 1994.

17. Joseph Sailer Jr. to Mary Lowber Sailer, April 26, 1942.

18. "18 Die as Airliner Hits Peak in Utah," *The New York Times*, May 2, 1942; "17 Bodies Removed from Plane Wreck," *The New York Times*, May 3, 1942.

19. Henrietta Vose to Joseph Sailer Jr., May 1942.

20. Joseph Sailer Jr. to Mary Lowber Sailer, Aug. 29, 1942.

21. Joseph Sailer Jr. to Mary Lowber Sailer, Sept. 27, 1942.

22. Tillman, *Dauntless Dive Bomber*, p. 9.

23. Archie Simpson, telephone interview with author, tape recording, May 21, 1994.

24. Joseph Sailer Jr. to Mary Lowber Sailer, Sept. 28, 1942.

Chapter Five

1. David Harcombe, *Solomon Islands: A Travel Survival Kit* (Hawthorn, Australia: Lonely Planet Publications, 1993).

2. Thomas G. Miller, *The Cactus Air Force* (New York: Harper & Row, 1969; reprint, Fredericksburg, Texas: The Admiral Nimitz Foundation, 1990), p. 17 (page citations are to the reprint edition).

3. Samuel B. Griffith II, *The Battle for Guadalcanal* (New York: J.B. Lippincott, 1963; reprint, New York: Bantam Books, 1980), p. 25 (page

citations are to the reprint edition).

4. Robert Sherrod, *History of Marine Corps Aviation in World War II* (Washington, D.C.: Combat Forces Press, 1952), pp. 63, 77, 433.

5. Griffith, *Battle for Guadalcanal*, p. 181. See also Sherrod, *Marine Corps Aviation*, p. 100.

6. Griffith, *Battle for Guadalcanal*, pp. 181–82; Sherrod, *Marine Corps Aviation*, p. 100.

7. Victor S. Falk, Jr., M.D., "A Marine Dive Bomber Squadron at Guadalcanal, 1942," *The Journal of Aviation Medicine* 24 (1953): pp. 237–48.

8. McEniry, *Marine Dive-Bomber Pilot*, p. 31; Howard Stanley, telephone interview by author, tape recording, June 7, 1994. The *Lurline* was built by the Bethlehem Shipbuilding Corp. of Quincy, Massachusetts. She was engaged in "deluxe California service" before the war, and was returned to cruising service after making numerous voyages as a troopship in the Pacific between 1942 and 1946. William A. Fox, "Monterey at Fifty-Seven," *Steamboat Bill* no. 189 (spring 1989): pp. 1–15; Roland W. Charles, *Troopships of World War II* (Washington, D.C.: The Army Transportation Association, n.d.).

9. VMSB-132 war diary.

10. Archie Simpson, telephone interview by author, tape recording, May 21, 1994.

11. Archie Simpson, interview by author, tape recording, Alexandria, Virginia, Oct. 11, 1993.

12. McEniry, *Marine Dive-Bomber Pilot*, p. 31.

13. McEniry, *Marine Dive-Bomber Pilot*, p. 32.

14. Richard B. Frank, *Guadalcanal: The Definitive Account of the Landmark Battle* (New York: Random House, 1990; reprint, New York: Penguin, 1992), p. 400 (page citations are to the reprint edition).

15. Howard Stanley to Mary Lowber Sailer, Aug. 5, 1946.

16. Louis B. Robertshaw, telephone interview by author, tape recording, June 2, 1994.

17. Louis E. Woods, interview transcript, Marine Corps Historical Center, Oral History Dept., p. 157; Falk, "Marine Dive Bomber Squadron."

18. McEniry, *Marine Dive-Bomber Pilot*, p. 51.

19. Falk, "Marine Dive Bomber Squadron."

20. Louis B. Robertshaw, telephone interview by author, tape recording, June 2, 1994.

21. Victor Falk, M.D., telephone interview by author, Jan. 3, 1994.

22. Louis B. Robertshaw, telephone interview by author, tape recording, June 2, 1994.

23. Edward Wallof, telephone interview by author, tape recording, June 13, 1994.

24. Howard Stanley, telephone interviews by author, tape recordings, Jan. 8, 1994, and June 7, 1994.

25. Archie Simpson, telephone interviews by author, tape recordings, Oct. 11, 1993, and May 21, 1994.

26. Other pilots, such as Archie "Hap" Simpson, rarely used the bomb sight, finding it cumbersome to fly without looking out the window. Archie Simpson, telephone interview by author, tape recording, May 21, 1994.

27. Other pilots, including Major Robertshaw, preferred simply to glance at the altimeter periodically during the dive. Louis B. Robertshaw, telephone interview by author, tape recording, June 2, 1994.

28. Archie Simpson, telephone interview by author, tape recording, May 21, 1994.

29. When the bomb was released, an arming wire was supposed to stay on the bomb rack, having slipped out through a hole in the bomb. If a crew upon its return found the arming wire was not still on the bomb rack, that indicated that the wire probably had gone with the bomb, and thus the bomb had not been armed. Archie Simpson, telephone interview by author, tape recording, May 21, 1994.

30. Other pilots, like Archie Simpson, only "grayed out," becoming light-headed but not losing consciousness. Archie Simpson, telephone interview by author, tape recording, May 21, 1994.

31. Howard Stanley, telephone interview by author, tape recording, Jan. 8, 1994.

32. Howard Stanley, telephone interviews by author, tape recordings, Jan. 8, 1994, and June 7, 1994.

33. John B. Lundstrom, *The First Team and the Guadalcanal Campaign: Naval Fighter Combat from August to November 1942* (Annapolis: Naval Institute Press, 1994), pp. 445, 450.

34. Sherrod, *Marine Corps Aviation*, p. 23.

35. McEniry, *Marine Dive-Bomber Pilot*, p. 170.

36. Edward Wallof, telephone interview by author, tape recording, June 13, 1994.

Chapter Six

1. Frank, *Guadalcanal*, p. 400.

2. Frank, *Guadalcanal*, p. 401.

3. Lundstrom, *Guadalcanal Campaign*, p. 471.

4. Frank, *Guadalcanal*, p. 428.

5. Frank, *Guadalcanal*, p. 429.

6. Frank, *Guadalcanal*, p. 435.

7. Lundstrom, *Guadalcanal Campaign*, p. 475. According to Lundstrom, the American Navy commanders found the likelihood of carriers in the area to be improbable, despite this report.

8. For a thorough account of this disaster, see Dan Kurzman, *Left to Die: The Tragedy of USS Juneau* (New York: Simon & Schuster, 1994; reprint, New York: Pocket Books, 1995).

9. Edwin P. Hoyt, *War in the Pacific, Volume III: South Pacific* (New York: Avon Books, 1991), p. 89.

10. Howard Stanley, telephone interviews by author, tape recordings, Jan. 8, 1994, and June 7, 1994.

11. Archie Simpson, telephone interview by author, tape recording, May 21, 1994.

12. Gordon W. Prange, *At Dawn We Slept: The Untold Story of Pearl Harbor* (New York: McGraw-Hill, 1981), pp. 322, 393.

13. Lundstrom, *Guadalcanal Campaign*, p. 477.

14. Miller, *Cactus Air Force*, p. 184.

15. Archie Simpson, telephone interview by author, tape recording, May 21, 1994.

16. Ibid.

17. Archie Simpson, interview by author, tape recording, Alexandria, Virginia, Oct. 11, 1993.

18. Lundstrom, *Guadalcanal Campaign*, p. 506; Miller, *Cactus Air Force*, p. 194.

19. McEniry, *Marine Dive-Bomber Pilot*, pp. 64–65.

20. Lundstrom, *Guadalcanal Campaign*, pp. 497–98.

21. Lundstrom, *Guadalcanal Campaign*, p. 499.

22. McEniry, *Marine Dive-Bomber Pilot*, p. 65.

23. Lundstrom, *Guadalcanal Campaign*, p. 500.

24. McEniry, *Marine Dive-Bomber Pilot*, p. 66.

25. Ibid.

26. Ibid.

27. Archie Simpson, telephone interview by author, tape recording, May 21, 1994.

28. It is unclear whether Sailer saw action on November 20. The war diary of VMSB-132 says that on that date Sailer "led an attack group composed of Lieutenants Eck, McEniry, Marshall, Janson and MTSgt. Gordon. This group accompanied by F4F's was out to hit a cargo transport and a destroyer, but was unable to make contact." However, Sailer's own log book shows no activity at all for November 18–22.

29. The war diary of Marine Air Group 14 says this action occurred on November 25, but that entry comes before the entry for November 23, and the November 25 date apparently is a typographical error.

30. Sailer's log book for November 25 lists his passenger's name as Ruffon.

31. McEniry, *Marine Dive-Bomber Pilot*, p. 79.

32. Richard G. Hubler and John A. DeChant, *Flying Leathernecks: The Complete Record of Marine Corps Aviation in Action 1941–1944* (Garden City, New York: Doubleday, Doran & Co., 1944), p. 92.

33. Ibid.; see also VMSB-132 war diary.

34. Jack Cram to Mary Lowber Sailer, Jan. 2, 1944; Sherrod, *Marine Corps Aviation*, p. 119.

35. Louis B. Robertshaw, telephone interview by author, tape recording, June 2, 1994.

36. Howard Stanley to Mary Lowber Sailer, May 5, 1949.

37. Jack Cram to Mary Lowber Sailer, Jan. 2, 1944; William Shields Jr. to Mary Lowber Sailer, Dec. 18, 1944.

38. The letter of Jack Cram to Sailer's mother on January 2, 1944, says that Sailer was to receive the sword from General Vandegrift as recognition for being the best dive-bomber pilot. McEniry, in *Marine Dive-Bomber Pilot* at pages v and 108, says Vandegrift awarded a Japanese sword to Lieutenant Charles Kollman of Sailer's squadron

on December 9, 1942 "for doing the most damage to the Japanese fleet." Archie Simpson, in an interview with the author on May 21, 1994, said both Sailer and Kollman were to receive Japanese swords at the ceremony.

39. William Shields, a Navy officer who served as one of the squadron's intelligence officers, wrote Sailer's mother that Sailer "told me that afternoon that he planned to appeal his assignment to field operations to Gen. Geiger the following day and in his mind the appointment was therefore still indefinite." William Shields to Mary Lowber Sailer, Dec. 18, 1944.

40. Louis B. Robertshaw, telephone interview by author, tape recording, June 2, 1994.

41. Sailer's brother John wrote to their mother with the following account, which recounts what John Sailer said he was told by John Lawrence, a Navy officer who served as an intelligence officer with Sailer's squadron:

> "Conditions became very muddled at the air fields, & it was deemed necessary to take drastic steps to remedy them. Joe was selected as the one hope to do the job & persuaded against his wishes <u>from the beginning</u> to take it over. On Dec. 7th he tried to report to Gen'l Woods, who wasn't available. He had been detached but unable to report. Then the report of the Jap ships came in. Lawrence said the pilots had always depended on Joe to lead them & Joe felt a great responsibility because no one else was around who had had a chance to take his place. As a result he went out."

> John Sailer to Mary Lowber Sailer, Aug. 13, 1943 (underlining in original).

42. Howard Stanley, telephone interview by author, tape recording, June 7, 1994.

43. No previously published accounts of Sailer's last flight, as far as I could determine, identified the gunner who accompanied him. As discussed in the text, some accounts erroneously stated that he had no gunner. The pilots and others I interviewed, including Sailer's regular gunner, Howard Stanley, did not know who the gunner was, but General Robertshaw made it clear that Sailer never would have gone on an attack mission without a gunner. The only solid evidence of the

gunner's name was the entry in Sailer's log book (see Appendix C), giving the last name of "Alexander." At the Marine Corps Historical Center at the Washington Navy Yard, a helpful historian, Robert Acquilina, looked through the index card file of Marine Corps casualty records for World War II for the name Alexander with a date of casualty of December 7, 1942. He quickly located the card of PFC James Woodward Alexander, born September 21, 1922, at Long Beach, California, listed as missing in action Dec. 7, 1942, at the Solomon Islands. When I showed Alexander's photograph and mentioned his full name to Howard Stanley and others, they still did not recognize him; he evidently was new to the Headquarters squadron of Marine Air Group 14. An inquiry to the National Personnel Records Center in St. Louis eventually yielded additional information about PFC Alexander's assignments, training, and awards.

44. Alexander's service records show that he attended "radio school," which is not the same as radio-gunner school. Howard Stanley, telephone interview by author, Sept. 7, 1994. Although it is not certain that Alexander received no training in aerial gunnery, there is no clear indication in the records that he did.

45. William Shields to Mary Lowber Sailer, Dec. 18, 1944.

46. United States Atlantic Fleet Attack Report, Dec. 7, 1942.

47. Frank, *Guadalcanal*, p. 520.

48. Christy Campbell, *Air War Pacific* (London: Reed International Books, 1990, reprint, New York: Crescent Books, 1990), p. 169 (page citation is to the reprint edition).

49. VMSB-132 war diary.

50. Archie Simpson, interview by author, tape recording, Alexandria, Virginia, Oct. 11, 1993.

51. Ibid.

52. The VMSB-132 war diary says the wounds were from .25-caliber bullets; the Pete float planes were armed with 7.7mm guns, whose ammunition would be the equivalent of .30-caliber. Assuming that the .25-caliber figure was an approximation, it appears that these figures provide some corroboration of the identity of the attacking planes.

Chapter Seven

1. Marine Air Group 14 war diary.
2. Archie Simpson, interview by author, tape recording, Alexandria, Virginia, Oct. 11, 1993.
3. McEniry, *Marine Dive-Bomber Pilot*, p. 80.
4. "Major Sailer's Squadron Helped Put Finishing Touches to Jap Battleship," *Philadelphia Evening Bulletin*, Nov. 28, 1942.
5. Foster Hailey, "Japanese Troops Died in Holocaust," *The New York Times*, Nov. 29, 1942.
6. Walter Canter, "Jap battleship sunk by Chestnut Hill ace," *Philadelphia Daily News*, Nov. 30, 1942.
7. "Maj. Sailer Aided in Convoy Rout," *Philadelphia Evening Bulletin*, Dec. 9, 1942.
8. For example, on December 10, 1942, the *Philadelphia Inquirer* ran a story headlined "U.S. Fliers Hit 4 Jap Warships." This story, by John M. McCullough, reported that one enemy "cruiser or large destroyer" was sunk and three other ships "were left blazing furiously" after an attack by American dive-bombers, torpedo-bombers, and fighters. However, although his family saved a clipping of this story and may have believed it involved him directly, it actually described action occurring on December 3, a day on which, according to his log book, Sailer did not fly.
9. Mrs. George Newhall to Mary Lowber Sailer, Jan. 15, 1942.
10. Louis B. Robertshaw to Mary Lowber Sailer, Jan. 19, 1943.
11. Col. John Dixon to Mary Lowber Sailer, March 2, 1943.
12. Lt. Gen. T. Holcomb to Mary Lowber Sailer, April 5, 1943.
13. Col. Emmett W. Skinner to Lawrence Litchfield Jr., April 15, 1943.
14. Martin Severson to Mary Lowber Sailer, April 24, 1943.
15. See, *e.g.*, Wilbur McCarty Jr., "Forty-Six Came Back," *The Leatherneck* (Oct. 1943): pp. 58–59. This article provides several accounts of dive-bomber pilots at Guadalcanal who survived for considerable periods of time after being shot down at sea. It includes the story of 2d Lt. Robert K. Meentz of Fort Madison, Iowa, and his gunner, Edward J. Withouski. These men, according to the article, got lost and landed in the water, where the plane floated for about forty seconds. Then they paddled about five miles to shore in a life raft, where a native

chief met them. After spending twenty-six days in the bush, they made their way back to the American forces.

General Louis B. Robertshaw, who had been Sailer's executive officer at Guadalcanal, confirmed that there was a good chance for a pilot to be rescued at sea: "Many a pilot was shot down and not recovered immediately, but later on, recovered. There was a good network of rescue in effect; not necessarily effective on water, but if one could get ashore, there were friendly coast watchers all along the island chain ... so if you didn't get killed on initial impact, you had a pretty good chance of surviving." Louis B. Robertshaw, telephone interview by author, tape recording, Oct. 21, 1993.

16. The text of the Navy Cross citation is set forth in full in Appendix C.

17. Floy Larsen to Mary Lowber Sailer, May 31, 1943.

18. Hilma Newman to Mary Lowber Sailer, July 3, July 6, and July 13, 1943.

19. Floy Larsen to Mary Lowber Sailer, June 6, 1944.

20. Hubler and DeChant, *Flying Leathernecks*, p. 93.

21. Hubler and DeChant, *Flying Leathernecks*, pp. 96–99. See also Lundstrom, *Guadalcanal Campaign*, pp. 509–11, 515–16.

22. Charles E. Kollman to Mary Lowber Sailer, June 13, 1944.

23. Jack Cram to Mary Lowber Sailer, Jan. 2, 1944.

24. Louis B. Robertshaw to Mary Lowber Sailer, Jan. 19, 1943.

25. Anne F. Dougherty to Mary Lowber Sailer, April 15, 1943.

26. Sailer's picture ran in the July 1943 issue of *The Marine Corps Gazette*, at page 50, along with the text of his Navy Cross commendation, but without any other information about his actions. The issue's masthead, at page 44, lists Colonel Clyde H. Metcalf, USMC, as editor.

27. Perceived inequities in the awarding of medals was a topic of some concern during World War II. For example, Captain Richard Hubler, co-author of *Flying Leathernecks*, noted in an article that achieved a fairly wide audience: "[W]hich is the more deserving of the Congressional Medal of Honor: a pilot who has shot down seven planes in a *tour de force* of twenty minutes or a pilot who has headed a squadron and borne its responsibilities for months of grueling air-sea-and-ground battle? The former got a Medal of Honor and the latter got the Navy Cross." Richard G. Hubler, "Winning Medals and Alienating People," *The Marine Corps Gazette* (Jan. 1944): pp. 55–56, quoted in *Time* (Jan. 24, 1944): p. 66.

28. Sherrod, *Marine Corps Aviation*, p. 425. The lone Marine Corps dive-bomber pilot to win the Medal of Honor was Captain Richard E. Fleming, who saw continuous action at Midway. Fleming was killed in that battle on June 5, 1942, when his SB2U was hit and burst into flames as he completed his bombing run against the heavy cruiser *Mikuma*, which later was sunk by other Marine and Navy pilots. Sherrod, *Marine Corps Aviation*, pp. 61–62.

29. "Major Sailer's Squadron Helped Put Finishing Touches to Jap Battleship," *Philadelphia Evening Bulletin*, Nov. 28, 1942.

30. Jack Cram to Mary Lowber Sailer, Jan. 2, 1944.

31. Ira Wolfert, "A Grandstand View of Jap Naval Disaster," *The Reader's Digest* 42 (Feb. 1943): pp. 11–16.

32. Ira Wolfert, *Battle for the Solomons* (Boston: Houghton Mifflin, 1943), pp. 149–72.

33. See, *e.g.*, Fletcher Pratt, "The Campaign for the Solomons: No. 3—Decision by Night," *Harper's Magazine* 188 (May 1944): pp. 564–76.

34. Hubler and DeChant, *Flying Leathernecks*, p. 87. The Main Line is an affluent area just outside Philadelphia, across the Schuylkill River, corresponding to what was the main line of the Pennsylvania Railroad. Many prominent Philadelphians have lived there over the years, but Sailer's family always lived within the city of Philadelphia.

35. Hubler and DeChant, *Flying Leathernecks*, p. 93.

36. Hubler and DeChant, *Flying Leathernecks*, p. 91.

37. Hubler and DeChant, *Flying Leathernecks*, p. 88.

38. Hubler and DeChant, *Flying Leathernecks*, p. 86.

39. Ibid.

40. William Shields to Mary Lowber Sailer, Dec. 18, 1944.

41. Jack Cram to Mary Lowber Sailer, Jan. 2, 1945.

42. Louis B. Robertshaw to Mary Lowber Sailer, Nov. 11, 1946.

43. George Dooley, interview by author, tape recording, Oct. 2, 1993.

44. Archie Simpson, telephone interview by author, tape recordingMay 21, 1994.

45. Ibid.

46. Louis B. Robertshaw, interview by author, tape recording, June 2, 1994.

47. Howard Stanley, letter to author, Aug. 1, 1994.

48. Lt. Col. H.S. Mazet, "Major Sailer: Flying Leatherneck," *Aircraft Age* 2 (June 1944): pp. 24–25, 58–59.

49. Sailer was to have his career memorialized in at least one other repository of popular culture. In an edition of *Wings Comics* that appeared at some point during or soon after the war, a monthly feature called "Air Heroes of World War II" featured a relatively factual account of the high points of his military service, complete with a series of illustrations with captions such as "Into the flak!!", "The Skipper scores", and "Bombs away!"

50. Col. Clyde H. Metcalf to Mary Lowber Sailer, Feb. 7, 1944.

51. The other medals were the American Defense Service medal, the Asiatic-Pacific Campaign medal, and the Victory Medal World War II. Col. L.S. Hamel, Marine Corps Headquarters, to Mary Lowber Sailer, Sept. 20, 1948.

Chapter Eight

1. McEniry, *Marine Dive-Bomber Pilot*, p. 80.

2. Louis B. Robertshaw, telephone interview with author, tape recording, June 2, 1994.

3. Howard Stanley, telephone interview with author, tape recording, June 7, 1994.

4. There is, understandably, a good deal of variation in reporting successful dive-bombing attacks. For example, it is difficult to distinguish hits from near-misses and it may be difficult to know which of several planes' bombs were the ones that hit. In any event, there were various summaries of Joe Sailer's accomplishments. John McEniry said: "He was credited with nine hits on ships in thirteen attacks—the best dive-bombing record of the war." McEniry, *Marine Dive-Bomber Pilot*, p. 116. The authors of *Flying Leathernecks* made this evaluation:

   "He was probably one of the greatest dive-bomber pilots this war has produced in the South Pacific, possibly in any, theater. . . . He scored perhaps a dozen hits, but he insisted on crediting most of them to other members of his squadron. His own record was four direct hits and four possibles plus uncounted near misses."

Hubler and DeChant, *Flying Leathernecks*, p. 86. Robert Sherrod rendered this summary:

> "[Sailer] contributed as much to the great November victory
> as any individual. In five weeks Major Sailer flew 25 missions,
> made contact with the enemy 19 times, dropped his bombs 12
> times, was credited with 6 hits and 3 near misses."

Sherrod, *Marine Corps Aviation*, p. 120. Sailer's Navy Cross citation, which covered only the period from November 10 to 15, 1942, credited him with "direct hits on a Japanese battleship of the Kongo Class, a heavy cruiser, a destroyer, and two transports." This record does not appear to be accurate, in view of the fact that his decision to fly one last mission on December 7 was motivated in part by his desire to finally hit a destroyer.

BIBLIOGRAPHY

Books

Buell, Harold L., *Dauntless Helldivers: A Dive-Bomber Pilot's Epic Story of the Carrier Battles*. New York: Orion Books, 1991; reprint, New York: Dell, 1992 (page citations are to the reprint edition).

Charle, Roland W., *Troopships of World War II*. Washington, D.C.: The Army Transportation Association, n.d.

Davies, R.E.G., *Pan Am: An Airline and its Aircraft*. New York: Orion Books, 1987.

Frank, Richard B., *Guadalcanal: The Definitive Account of the Landmark Battle*. New York: Random House, 1990; reprint, New York: Penguin Books, 1992 (page citations are to the reprint edition).

Gannon, Michael, *Operation Drumbeat: The Dramatic True Story of Germany's First U-Boat Attacks Along the American Coast in World War II*. New York: Harper & Row, 1990, reprint, New York: Harper Perennial, 1991 (page citations are to the reprint edition).

Griffith, Samuel B. II, *The Battle for Guadalcanal*. New York: J.B. Lippincott, 1963; reprint, New York: Bantam Books, 1980 (page citations are to the reprint edition).

Hague, Arnold, *Destroyers for Great Britain: A History of the 50 Town Class Ships Transferred from the United States to Great Britain in 1940*. Annapolis: Naval Institute Press, 1990.

Hammel, Eric, *Guadalcanal: Decision at Sea: The Naval Battle of Guadalcanal, November 13–15, 1942*. New York: Crown, 1988.

Harcombe, David, *Solomon Islands: A Travel Survival Kit*. Hawthorn, Australia: Lonely Planet Publications, 1993.

Hoyt, Edwin P., *War in the Pacific, Volume III: South Pacific*. New York: Avon Books, 1991.

Hubler, Richard G. & John A. DeChant, *Flying Leathernecks: The Complete Record of Marine Corps Aviation in Action 1941–1944*. Garden City, New York: Doubleday, Doran & Co., Inc., 1944.

Johnson, Edward C., *Marine Corps Aviation: The Early Years 1912–1940*. Washington, D.C.: History & Museums Division, United States Marine Corps, 1977.

Joseph, Franklin, *Letters Home from Britain at War*. New York: privately published, 1942.

Keegan, John, *The Second World War*. New York: Penguin Books, 1990.

Kurzman, Dan, *Left to Die: The Tragedy of the USS Juneau*. New York: Simon & Schuster, 1994; reprint, Pocket Books, 1995.

Lundstrom, John B., *The First Team and the Guadalcanal Campaign: Naval Fighter Combat from August to November 1942*. Annapolis: Naval Institute Press, 1994.

McEniry, John Howard, Jr., *A Marine Dive-Bomber Pilot at Guadalcanal*. Tuscaloosa: The University of Alabama Press, 1987.

Mersky, Peter B., *U.S. Marine Corps Aviation: 1912 to the Present*. Baltimore: The Nautical & Aviation Publishing Company of America, 1983, reprint with revisions, 1987 (page citations are to the reprint edition).

Millay, Norma, ed., *Letters of Edna St. Vincent Millay*. New York: Harper & Brothers, 1952.

Miller, Thomas G., *The Cactus Air Force*. New York: Harper & Row, 1969; reprint, Fredericksburg, Texas: The Admiral Nimitz Foundation, 1990 (page citations are to the reprint edition).

Moran, John B., *Creating a Legend: The Complete Record of Writing About the United States Marine Corps*. Chicago: Moran/Andrews, Inc., 1973.

Prange, Gordon W., *At Dawn We Slept: The Untold Story of Pearl Harbor*. New York: McGraw-Hill, 1981.

Prange, Gordon W., *Miracle at Midway*. New York: McGraw Hill, 1982; reprint, New York: Penguin Books, 1983.

Reserve Officers of Public Affairs Unit 4-1, *The Marine Corps Reserve: A History*. Washington, D.C.: United States Marine Corps, 1966.

Robinson, Reuel, *History of Camden and Rockport Maine*. Camden, Maine: Camden Publishing Co., 1907.

St. John, Philip A., *Bombardier: A History*. Paducah, Kentucky: Turner Publishing Co., 1993.

Sherrod, Robert, *History of Marine Corps Aviation in World War II*. Washington, D.C.: Combat Forces Press, 1952.

Smith, Peter C., *The History of Dive Bombing*. Annapolis: Nautical & Aviation Publishing Co., 1981.

Stern, Rob, *SBD Dauntless in Action*. Carrollton, Texas: Squadron/Signal Publications, 1984.

Taylor, Barry, *Pan American's Ocean Clippers*. Blue Ridge Summit, PA: Tab Books, 1991.

Tillman, Barrett, *The Dauntless Dive Bomber of World War II*. Annapolis: Naval Institute Press, 1976.

Willock, Roger, *Unaccustomed to Fear*. Princeton, NJ: privately published, 1968.

Winston, Robert A., *Dive Bomber: Learning to Fly the Navy's Fighting Planes*. New York: Holiday House, 1939; facsimile reprint, Annapolis: Naval Institute Press, 1991.

Wolfert, Ira, *Battle for the Solomons*. Boston: Houghton-Mifflin, 1943.

Wolfert, Ira, *Torpedo 8: The Attack and Vengeance of Swede Larsen's Bomber Squadron*. Boston: Houghton-Mifflin, 1943.

Articles

Falk, Victor S., Jr., "A Marine Dive Bomber Squadron at Guadalcanal, 1942." *The Journal of Aviation Medicine* 24 (June 1953): 237–39, 248.

Fox, William A., "Monterey at Fifty-Seven." *Steamboat Bill* no. 189 (Spring 1989): 4–15.

Hubler, Captain Richard G., "Winning Medals and Alienating People." *The Marine Corps Gazette* (January 1944): 55–56.

Mazet, Lt. Col. H.S., "Major Sailer, Flying Leatherneck." *Aircraft Age* 2, no. 5 (June 1944): 24–25, 57–59.

McCarty, Milburn, Jr., "Forty-Six Came Back." *The Leatherneck* (October 1943): 58–59.

"Mechanical Brains: Working in Metal Boxes, Computing Devices Aim Guns and Bombs with Inhuman Accuracy." *Life* 16, no. 4 (Jan. 24, 1944): 66–72.

Morale. *Time* (Jan. 24, 1944): 66.

Pratt, Fletcher, "The Campaign for the Solomons: No. 3—Decision by Night." *Harper's Magazine* 188, no. 1128 (May 1944): 564–76.

Searle, Loyd, "The Bombsight War: Norden vs. Sperry." *IEEE Spectrum* (September 1989): 60–64.

Wolfert, Ira, "A Grandstand View of Jap Naval Disaster." *Reader's Digest* 42, no. 250 (February 1942): 11–16.

Other Materials

Arnold, Gen. H.H. Papers. Diary of Trip to England, April, 1941. Library of Congress Manuscript Room.

Experiences in England. 16mm, 45 min. Sperry Gyroscope Co., Brooklyn, N.Y., 1943.

Persons Contacted Directly

Arvid Blackmun	Alice Lingelbach
William Campbell	Jack Long
John Condon	Richard L. Murray
George Dooley	John L. Pool
John Elliott	Warren Roberge
Endsley P. Fairman	Louis B. Robertshaw
Victor Falk	John Shepp
Carl A. Frische	Archie Simpson
Howard J. Fuller	Howard Stanley
George Herlihy	Charles Stephenson
Franklin Joseph	John H. Stock
Mary Lowber Knight	Edward J. Wallof
Tom Liggett	Priscilla Wilson

INDEX

A

Abington Memorial Hospital, 20
Agua Caliente Golf and Country
  Club, 28
Agua Caliente Jockey Club, 27, 28
Ahoskie, North Carolina, 79
Air Ministry, British, 57, 134, 147n.
Aircraft Age, 125
Aircraft One, First Marine
  Brigade, 35
Alexander, James Woodward, 104,
  106, 156n.
Arnold, Henry "Hap," 56, 59, 148n.
Auka Harbor, 102
Australia, 72
Autogiro, 19–20, 142n.
Autopilot, 44–45, 58, 66, 148n.

B

B-17 bomber, 46, 53, 58
B-24E bomber, 59
Bald Rock, 12
Battle for Guadalcanal, The, 74
Battle of Britain, 45, 50–51
Battle of Cape Esperance, 78
Battle of Savo Island, 77
Battle of the Eastern Solomons, 77
Battle of the Santa Cruz Islands,
  78, 91
Bauer, Harold W., 115

Baum, Horace C. Jr., 89, 90
Benz factory, 58, 134, 148n.
Boeing School of Aeronautics, 31,
  32
Bomb sight, xi, 44–49, 52, 53,
  57–60, 85, 133–35, 147–49n.
Bombardiers, Inc., xiii
Bonnat, Léon, 18
Boscombe Down, 51, 53, 57, 58,
  133–34, 146n., 148n.
Bowen, Ivor, 52, 146n.
Brenner, Ernie, 81
Bright, Cruger L. "Curley," 90, 92,
  96
British Solomon Islands Protec-
  torate, 72
Brooklyn, New York, 41, 43, 44,
  114
Brunk, Paul, 26, 27

C

"Cactus Air Force," 73, 80, 88, 94,
  96, 97, 127
Camden, Maine, 8–13, 21, 22,
  25–26, 61, 63
Camden, New Jersey, 35
Camp Miramar, California, 68
Camp Wheeler, Georgia, 7
Campbell, Thomas, 56
Cape Esperance, 91

Carroll, Bill, 23
Casablanca (movie), 147n.
Chase, Frances, 32
Chase, Margaret, 32
Chase, Mrs., 31–32
Chesapeake Bay, 3
Chestnut Hill Academy, xiv, 14
China, 125
Chloride, Arizona, 30
Christian, Frank, 105
Churchman, Elizabeth (born Sailer), 9, 62, 128
Churchman, Emily, *see* Starr, Emily
Cierva, Juan de la, 142n.
Coastwatchers, 73, 82, 103, 158n.
Cochran, Jackie, 43
Cooley, Albert D., 109
Cram, Jack, 115, 116, 119, 122
Crozer, Marion, 36, 69
Curtiss F6C, 22
Curtiss-Wright Airport, Valley Stream, Long Island, 21

D
Davis, Bobby, 27
DC-3, 48, 55–56
DeChant, John A., 114–15, 122
Delaware River, 3, 35
Denton, Tom, 30
Depression, 21, 30
Destroyers-for-bases deal (*see* Lend Lease), 45–46, 48
Dooley, George, 94, 96, 123
Dougherty, Anne F., 117
Dougherty, Robert E. Jr., 116
Douglas Aircraft Company, 65
Dow, Commander, 56
Doylestown & Easton Motorcoach Company, 30

Drexel University, 6
Dyce, Scotland, 57, 134

E
Eastern Shore, Maryland, 2
Eck, Walter A., 88, 92, 154n.
El Segundo, California, 65
Elkton, Maryland, 3
England, 45–60, 64, 66–67, 72
Espiritu Santo, 77, 89, 103
Esval, O.E., 45
Evarts, Lieutenant, 89
"Experiences in England" (movie), xiv, 58, 66–67, 128

F
F4F, 96, 97, 105–06, 115
Falk, Victor, 81
Farnborough, England, 50–52, 55
"Fighting Marines" (comic strip), 126
First Marine Air Wing, 103
First Marine Aircraft Group, 61
First Marine Division, 73, 77, 103
Fleming, Richard E., 159n.
Floyd Bennett Field, 39, 43
Flying Leathernecks, 114–16, 119–125
Ford automobile, 26, 31
Forecastle, 10, 11, 13
Foss, Joe, 114–15, 128
Fox, William J., 102
Fresno, California, 33
Freuler, Herbert, 32
Frische, Carl A., xiv, 42, 45, 47, 58

G
Gavutu, 73
Geiger, Roy, 103, 155n.

168

Gordon, Kenneth, 89, 90, 92, 95, 98, 154n.
Griffith, Samuel, 74
Grumman J 2F, 102
Guadalcanal,ix–xii, 66, 71–106, 108, 109–10, 116, 119–23, 125, 127, 129, 131
Gyrocompass, 44
Gyroscope, 43–44

H

HMS *Lincoln*, 49, 145–46n.
Hagan, Walter, 29
Hailey, Foster, 109
Halifax, Nova Scotia, 46, 48, 49
Halsey, William F. Jr., 78
Harcum, William, 39
Haruna, 74
Hawk fighter, 22
Heist, 24–25, 143n.
Henderson Field, 73–75, 77–80, 82–83, 86–88, 92–100, 102, 107, 120
Henderson, Lofton R., 73
Herlihy, George B. "Jug," 89, 98, 99
Hermann Goering Tank Works, 59
Herrick, Donald, 105–06
Hiei, 92–95, 107, 109, 119
High-altitude bombing, 53
Hogan, Ben, 29
Holcomb, Thomas, 110
Hong Kong, 71
Hronek, William, 92
Hubler, Richard G., 115, 122

I

IBM, 126
Indian Rights Association, 18
Iron Hill, Maryland, 3

J

Jamestown, Rhode Island, 8, 10
Janson, Russell, 89, 90, 94, 154n.
Joseph, Eleanor, 41
Joseph, Franklin, xiv, 41, 52, 54–55, 56, 146n.
Junyo, 92

K

Kelley, Priscilla (born Sailer), xiv, 9, 11
Kelly, Robert E., 95, 96, 98
Keystone Battery, 6
Kinugasa, 96
Kirishima, 92
Knight, Mary Lower (born Sailer), ix, 8, 11, 12, 13, 14, 23, 42
Kokumbona, 99
Kollman, Charles E., 89, 93, 94, 95, 98, 100, 105, 116, 155n.
Kolumbangara Island, 100
Kongo, 74

L

La Guardia Airport, 48, 56
Lafayette, Marquis de, 3
Lake Megunticook, 10, 12
Lake Tahoe, 32
Lambeti Plantation, 100
Larkin, 28
Larsen, Floy, xv, 62, 114–15, 126
Larsen, Harold H. "Swede," 89
Lawrence, John, 122, 155n.
Lend Lease, 46
Lingelbach, Alice (born Sailer), xiv, 8, 13, 30, 42, 128
Litchfield, Lawrence, 42, 112
Litchfield, Mary, *see* Reid, Mary

Litchfield, Priscilla, *see* Wilson, Priscilla
Lloyd, William, 6
Lockheed Hudson bomber, 46, 48, 52, 53, 57–58, 133, 147n.
London, England, 50–51, 54, 55, 67
Los Angeles, California, 31, 104
Lowber, Edward, 141n.
Lundstrom, John, xv, 96
Lunga River, 104, 122
Lurline, 75, 151n.

M
Main Line, 36, 120, 159n.
Malaria, 80
Mallinson, John, 57, 59–60, 133, 135, 148n.
Marine Air Group 14, 104, 107, 130, 154n.
Marine Corps Gazette, 118
Maryland, 2–3
Matson steamship line, 75
Mazet, Horace, 36
McBryde, E.P., 105
McEniry, John H. Jr., x, 66, 89, 94, 96–99, 101, 104, 105, 108, 129, 154n.
Medal of Honor, 118–19, 158n.
Medford, Oregon, 33–34
Meentz, Robert K., 157n.
Megunticook Golf Club, 11
Messerschmitt 110, 52, 67
Metcalf, Clyde H., 118, 127, 158n.
Mexico, 26, 27
Midway Island, 71, 159n.
Mikuma, 159n.
Millay, Edna St. Vincent, 13–14, 141n.
Millay, Kathleen, 13
Millay, Norma, 13, 141n.

"Millimeter Mike," 74
Mitsubishi F1M1 "Pete," 105–06, 156n.
Monocoupe, 33
Mount Battie, 10, 12, 26
Mount Megunticook, 12, 13
Munda Island, 101

N
Naval Battle of Guadalcanal, 92–100, 108–110, 123
Navy Cross, 112, 114, 117–18, 127, 139, 158n., 161n.
Navy Scouting 4, 100
New Bern, North Carolina, 61
New Britain, 74
New Caledonia, 76
New England summer homes, 2
New Georgia Island, 88, 100, 101, 105, 106, 107, 131
New Georgia Sound, 72
New Hebrides, 77
New York World's Fair, 42
New York City, 31, 56, 67
Newhall, Mrs., 111
Newlin, Ledlie, 36
Newman, Hilma, 41, 114
Norden bomb sight, 45, 59, 85, 135, 149n.
Norden, Carl, 45
North Bay, New Georgia, 105
North Island, San Diego, 63
Noumea, 76

O
Oakland, California, 31

P
P-39, 89, 97

Pan American World Airways, 38, 55, 56–57
Clipper, 55–57
Panama Canal, 31
Panama Pacific Line, 31
Pearce, Group Captain, 48
Pearl Harbor, 62, 68, 71, 93, 104
Penobscot Bay, 10
Pensacola, 22, 36, 38, 39
Peterson, 26
Phar Lap, 27, 28
Philadelphia Athletics, 26
Philadelphia, 2, 3, 4, 8, 11, 14, 18, 25, 33, 35, 68, 120, 159n.
Philippines, 71
"Pistol Pete," 80
Pitcairn, Harold, 142n.
Pool, Lieutenant, 105
Pratt & Whitney, 33
Princeton University, xiv, 15, 21, 120, 131
Public Records Office, xvi

Q
Quadrangle Club, 15
Quantico, Virginia, x, 35, 61–63, 114

R
R4D, 77
Rabaul, 74
Ralston, 29
Reid, Mary (born Litchfield), 42, 64
"Renascence," 13
Renner, Joe, 114
Revolutionary War, 3
Richard, Robert H., 94
Robertshaw, Louis B., xiii, 68, 76, 79, 89, 92, 94–96, 98, 104, 108, 111, 116, 123, 124, 129, 152n., 156n., 158n.

Rockledge, 9, 11
Roosevelt, Franklin D., 45, 46
Roosevelt, Theodore, 12
Rosereta Beach, Mexico, 26
Royal Air Force, 46, 48, 50, 52, 54, 57–60, 133–35, 147n.
Royal Canadian Air Force, 48
Royal Canadian Navy, 145n.
Royal Navy, 48
Royal Norwegian Navy, 146n.

S
Sailer & Stevenson, 6
Sailer, Albin, 11
Sailer, Albin Penington, 9, 25
Sailer, Alice, *see* Lingelbach, Alice
Sailer, Anne West, 9
Sailer, Elizabeth, *see* Churchman, Elizabeth
Sailer, Emily (sister of Joseph Sailer Jr.), 8
Sailer, Emily (born Woodward), 7
Sailer, John (brother of Joseph Sailer Jr.), 9, 11, 12, 29, 36, 37, 69, 108, 128
Sailer, John (grandfather of Joseph Sailer Jr.), 6–7
Sailer, Joseph (father of Joseph Sailer Jr.), 6–9, 11, 13, 16–18
Sailer, Joseph (great-grandfather of Joseph Sailer Jr.), 6
Sailer, Joseph Jr.
ancestors, 2–8
aviator's log book, xi, 137–38, 154n., 157n.
birth, 8
childhood, 8–15
college years, 15–17
death, 106
diary, 24

family, 8–14, 16–20
final flight, 103–06, 155n.
flight training, 21–28
letters of, xi
Navy Cross, 112, 114, 117–18,
    127, 139
personal papers, xi
physical stature, 14, 80
promotions in rank, 25, 35, 37, 67
reactions to accidents and crises,
    32, 34–35, 42–43, 106, 131
reputation as dive-bomber
    pilot, 1, 130, 160n.
service as flight instructor, 36, 54
service at Guadalcanal, ix,
    76–106, 154n.
telegrams notifying of his loss,
    110–12
trip to England, xi–xii, 47–60
typical dive-bombing mission,
    82–87, 130–31
Sailer, Mary, *see* Knight, Mary
    Lowber
Sailer, Mary Lowber (born Straw-
    bridge), xi, 2, 5, 8, 9; 11, 13, 18,
    19, 27, 108–117, 121, 127–28
Sailer, Nancy, 24
Sailer, Priscilla, *see* Kelley, Priscilla
Sailer, Virginia, 9
San Diego, 26, 31, 63, 65, 75, 78,
    102, 108, 111
San Francisco, 31, 67
Sandretto, Amedeo, 89
Santa Ana (island, Solomon
    Islands), 72
Santa Catalina (island, Solomon
    Islands), 72
Santa Isabel (island, Solomon
    Islands), 72
Sarazen, Gene, 29

Savo Island, 105, 107
SB2U-3 Vindicator, 63, 65
SBD Dauntless, 65–66, 68, 74, 78–79,
    82–90, 92–106, 125–26, 129
Schanlin, General, 56
Severson, Martin A., 27, 29, 36, 113
Shields, William, 104, 121, 155n.
Simpson, Archie "Hap," xiii, 76,
    89, 90, 93, 95–96, 98–99, 102,
    105–06, 108, 123, 152n.
Singapore, 71
Sioux Indians, 18
Skinner, John, 96, 98, 99, 101
"Slot, the," 72, 74, 83, 88, 105
Solomon Islands, 71–73, 80, 110
Spalding, Emmy, 27
Spang, William F., 102
Sperry Gyroscope Company, xi,
    xiv, 1, 38–39, 41–48, 51, 53–54,
    56–60, 66–67, 85, 120, 128, 135,
    147n., 149n.
Sperry, Elmer Ambrose, 44
Sperzel, John E., 89
Spring Bank, 4–5, 14, 108
"Stairstepping," 83–84
Stanley, Howard, xiii, 78–79,
    82–83, 85–87, 93, 101, 103–04,
    124, 128, 129, 155n.
Starr, Emily (born Churchman),
    110
Stephenson, Charles, 15–16
Strawbridge, Alice Welsh, 3–5, 9,
    11, 18
Strawbridge, Anne West, 11,
    19–20, 142n.
Strawbridge, George, 3, 5, 9
Strawbridge, John, 2, 3
Strawbridge, John Jr., 14, 15, 19
Sullivan, Lieutenant, 89
Swim fins, 61, 63, 149n.

T

Tassafaronga, 91
Taylor Cub, 33
TBF Avenger, 83, 89, 94, 97
Thorney Island, England, 58, 134
Tijuana, Mexico, 26
Tinsley, Frank, 126
"Tokyo Express," 73, 88, 91
Tontouta, 77
Tulagi, 73
Tunibuli, 88
Tyboron Harbor, Denmark, 57, 133, 147n.

U

USS *Enterprise*, 78, 91
USS *Hornet*, 78, 89, 91
USS *Juneau*, 92
USS *Mumu*, 75
USS *Portland*, 93
USS *Yarnall*, 49
U-boats, 48
Unisys Corporation, 44
United Air Lines, 31, 33, 35, 67, 120
United States
    aid to England, 45–46
    entry into World War II, 59, 135
United States Marine Corps, 7, 21, 29, 35, 38, 47, 54, 65, 110, 112–13
University of Pennsylvania, 7, 32

V

Vandegrift, A.A., 103, 154n.
VMF-212, 115
VMJ-152, 104
VMSB-131, 61, 94, 96
VMSB-132, 64–69, 75–90, 92–106, 107–08, 116, 124, 129, 154n., 156n.
VMSB-141, 75, 80, 81, 89, 95, 99

VMSB-142, 97, 98, 99, 105
VMSB-241, 73
Vose, Frederic Blin, 48–53, 57–58, 66–67, 128
Vose, Frederic H.E., 67
Vose, Henrietta, 67
Vose, Jane, 67
Vought O2U Corsair, 22
VT-8, 89
VT-10, 94

W

Waco biplane, 16, 131
Wadi-al-Canar, 72
Wake Island, 71
Walker, Lucy, 142n.
Wallof, Edward, 64, 89, 90, 99, 105
Wasatch Mountains, 67
"Washing Machine Charlie," 80
Washington, George, 3
Watson, Jane, 126
Watson, Thomas, 126
Webb, James, 39, 144n.
Welsh, Herbert, 18–19
Welsh, John, 4, 18, 141n.
Welsh, Mary Lower, 141n.
White, William, 42, 63
Wildcat fighters, 75
Wilderness, The, 5, 14
William Penn Charter School, 14
Wilmington, Delaware, 3
Wilson, Priscilla (born Litchfield), xvi, 42
Woods, Louis, 103, 155n.

XYZ

Yankee Clipper, 55
Yudachi, 93
Zero, 86, 88, 89, 105, 118
Zimmerman, 22